CUSTOMERS ARE THE AGENDA

Books are to be returned on or before

the last date below

7/4/22		
28/4/22		

For a complete list of Management Books 2000 titles
visit our website on http://www.mb2000.com

CUSTOMERS ARE THE AGENDA

A practical guide to customer-centric management

Stephen Hewett

2000

The extracts from J.B. Priestley's *An Inspector Calls* and *The Good Companions* are reprinted by permission of United Agents on behalf of: The Estate of J.B. Priestley.

First published in 2013 by Management Books 2000 Ltd
36 Western Road
Oxford OX1 4LG
Tel: 0044 (0) 1865 600738
Email: info@mb2000.com
Web: www.mb2000.com

British Library Cataloguing in Publication Data is available

ISBN 9781852527181

CONTENTS

ACKNOWLEDGEMENTS

Once again for my second book my sincere thanks to all the people in my life who help me enjoy being customer-centric. These people include my wife Carolyn, my daughter Dee, my son Alex, my son-in-law James and, my two wonderful grandsons Aaron and Ryan. I also draw much inspiration from my colleagues, especially David Pickering, Kevin Waters, Graham Simmons, Steve Nolan, Allan Barr and my business partner Melvyn Lesser; and from my clients, particularly Perry Price and Steve Carson at Argos, who have shown that customer-centricity can be made to work in the largest of organisations.

From my days at the John Lewis Partnership, I would like to extend my thanks to Luke Mayhew. From my aviation days, my gratitude to David Fairclough, who taught me how to be an excellent pilot and started me down the road of understanding people.

In the UK, my sincere gratitude to Helen Stevens and Katy Hall of ITV plc, Mark Price of Waitrose; Professor David Thomson and David Howlett of MMR Research; and Steve Lewis and Donna Morrison of Majestic Wine.

I would in addition once again like to thank James Essinger for his more than comprehensive assistance and talents. Many thanks also to Barbara Lammers, Michael A. Folkes, to Yvonne Whiteman for the excellent job she did of the copy-editing, Maurice Lyon for proof-reading the manuscript and to Fiona Godfrey for her help with word-processing.

Finally, my sincere gratitude to my publisher, Nick Dale-Harris, for his enthusiastic response to my first book and to this second one, and for all his help and guidance since then.

FOREWORD
by Perry Price, Operations Manager, Argos

I was delighted when Stephen Hewett asked me whether I would write a foreword for this book.

Anyone in business today must not only put the customer first but must take every effort to see the world from the customer's point of view. It's only when you have a real empathy and understanding of customers and their needs and perspectives that you can hope to meet customer expectations and also ideally to exceed them.

Stephen has helped Argos generate a paradigm shift in how we see our customers. We used to, in effect, hand out edicts from head office to our branch managers; edicts we believed would maximise the quality of our customer service. I'm not saying all these edicts were inaccurate in what they tried to do, but the point was that they issued from the top of the organisation rather than being generated and created within the branches *by the very people who dealt with customers on a day-to-day basis.*

When I met Stephen, I realised I'd encountered someone who was talking and thinking about customers in a way no-one ever had before, at least no-one I'd met.

For Stephen, being customer-centric is not just something you do in business because you want to make money! No, for Stephen, customer-centricity is a deep and wide-ranging business philosophy that he actually extends to all of life.

Stephen also taught me that the way any organisation sees a customer needs to be, in effect, *a bloodline that runs throughout the entire organisation.* Yes, of course, organisations have administrative things to do as well as working directly with customers, but they can only succeed in today's highly competitive business environments if their entire focus is around what the customer needs.

In order to generate that focus on customers, there really is no alternative but for the organisation to take every possible step at a grass-roots level to find out what customers are thinking and feeling, and what they want the organisation to do that it's not doing now.

Another problem is that the larger an organisation becomes, the more remote the organisation may find itself getting from its customers, whether culturally and often also logistically and geographically.

This happens partly because large organisations frequently think they have to be highly centralised to operate at maximum efficiency.

Yet it's not just that which is the problem, but also that there is a tendency for executives in a big organisation to become too engrossed emotionally and professionally with internal political goings-on at the organisation's head office, rather than thinking about customers and what customers need.

Reader, believe me, this short, highly-focused book you're about to read is full to the brim with sensible, workable, practical advice for how to win the hearts and minds of your customers, and how to put your customers first. There are no cunning tricks in the book; every tip is logical, sensible and in the final analysis, also honourable.

At Argos, we've benefited enormously from allowing

Stephen's philosophy of customer service to inform and guide our initiatives.

As a result of his advice and help, we've conducted a full review of the business and now have what we believe is a first-rate ongoing dialogue with customers. We still have things to do to ensure that our entire organisation is completely focused culturally, strategically and tactically around our customers and their needs. But already every store manager in our organisation knows that he or she has absolute carte blanche to deliver the best service the branch can, and that we are supporting that delivery in every conceivable respect.

In essence, what Stephen has helped us do is to allow everyone at Argos to be brilliant with customers. I hope this excellent book will help you to be brilliant with customers too!

PREFACE

This book aims to provide you with 30 reliable, tried and tested tips to help you win the hearts and minds of your customers.

The tips apply whatever your professional activity might be, and whoever your customers are and wherever they are located. The tips also apply whether you refer to your customers as *customers* or *clients.*

I started my career in aviation, beginning as a commercial pilot and then moving into a management role. Subsequently I decided to move into the world of retailing. I joined the John Lewis Partnership (JLP), starting out literally on the shopfloor. I spent fifteen years at the JLP, and was deeply influenced there in my thinking, not only about business but also about life, by the strong emphasis that the JLP puts on its customers.

In particular, I was much influenced by the JLP philosophy of 'VASH', which means giving customers the following:

- **Value** – Value for money.

- **Assortment** – Fundamental to the JLP philosophy is their belief that customers must be offered a wide range of buying choices. This means a wide assortment of merchandise and also a wide range of options (size, colour and other variables) within a particular product range.

- **Service** – Customer service. The JLP philosophy is, simply, that everything that can be done to maximise the quality of customer service, must be done.

- **Honesty** – Honesty in how customers are treated. During the training course I attended just after I joined the JLP, a woman on the course asked the trainer what we should do if, for example, a lady customer comes to try on a dress which the sales assistant thinks looks awful on her, but she – the customer – likes. 'Should we conceal what we really feel,' the trainee asked, 'and tell her that the dress looks great on her?' The trainer said emphatically that no, not telling the truth to customers was unacceptable. Instead, the sales assistant should suggest some other dresses which look better on her, and should if necessary point out why the dress does not suit her as well as she thinks it does.

In 2000, after I left the JLP – by which time I was a development manager in charge of research and expansion – I went to work for the publicly-listed information technology and business consultancy Charteris, where I am still an associate partner. I am now also involved as founding partner of C3 Partners, which specialises in helping organisations both in the private and public sectors streamline themselves for maximum customer-centricity.

I've spent all my career focusing on customer-centricity, though admittedly it's only been in the past five years that I've consciously used the term 'customer-centricity' in my professional practice. By the way, I didn't invent the term, and it's not clear who did. The term seems to have come into being around the end of the twentieth century. By the first decade of the twenty-first century, the term 'customer-centricity' was starting to be used more frequently to describe the process of making an organisation more customer-focused.

'Customer-centricity' is certainly spoken of today by an increasingly large number of professionals in all vertical markets, both in the private and public sectors. They believe it represents the way ahead for all organisations that:

- really care about their customers
- want to put that feeling of caring into practice.

However, there hasn't been much effort to define what 'customer-centricity' means. So let me try to redress that balance. I see customer-centricity as:

- a way of thinking for your professional life
- a business strategy.

As a way of thinking in your professional life, customer-centricity can be seen as *the philosophy of empathising fully with your customer's agenda, to deliver the best mutually beneficial outcome for that customer and for you.*

As a business strategy, customer-centricity can be seen as *the process of ensuring that every individual and department within an organisation is taking all feasible steps to add value to what the organisation does for its customers.*

I truly believe that customer-centricity can only be implemented successfully when you believe in it with all your heart. It's a human thing, a real thing, and it needs sincerity and a genuine sense of warmth towards customers if it is going to be implemented successfully.

We can learn a good deal about how to implement customer-centricity by contemplating the fate of Customer Relationship Management (CRM), a highly popular business strategy during much of the 1990s.

CRM was sold by computer software companies as add-on software which was supposed to give organisations new levels of support in their customer service initiatives.

As such, CRM didn't really work. The software more or less did what it was supposed to do, but organisations implementing it were disappointed to find that even after they'd installed the software and got it working, the quality of customer service wasn't revolutionised as a result.

But how could it be? After all, if customer-centricity was something you could just install by loading a programme or following a set procedure, everyone would have it and there would be no need for me to write this book.

But the very fact that customers are frequently dissatisfied with the level of service they receive proves that customer-centricity is far from being something that everyone has.

Ultimately, customer-centricity is delivered not by an organisation but by the organisation's employees. Whether you choose to see customer-centricity primarily as a personal philosophy or as a business strategy – and as you'll see from what I've written above, I believe it's both – customer-centricity can effect a massively positive revolution in your organisation, no matter how well your organisation is doing.

Even more importantly, customer-centricity can have enormous potential as a personal philosophy. As **Tip 13** makes clear, if you truly are a disciple of customer-centricity, you won't want to leave it behind when you leave your workplace! The truth is that customer-centricity can infuse every area of your life with fresh delight and create opportunities that you may never have dreamed would come along.

All work, ultimately, is done for a customer and so it's no exaggeration to say that selling things to customers is the basis of all human economic activity. So focusing on customer-centricity is not something you have an option about. If you want your life to be all it can be, if you want to contribute to the world, being customer-centric is something you *need* to be.

The truth is that customer-centricity is a way of life, one that can bring enormous benefits to your career, your personal life and your entire outlook on the world.

Stephen Hewett,
London

KEY DEFINITIONS

Customer-centricity as a way of thinking in your professional life:

The philosophy of empathising fully with your customer's agenda to deliver the best mutually beneficial outcome for that person and for you.

Customer-centricity as a business strategy:

The process of ensuring that every individual and department within an organisation is taking all steps to add value to what the organisation does for its customers.

Note that customers can be either *external* to your organisation (meaning consumers and end-users of products and services), or *internal* (meaning that they work within your organisation). Internal customers might include a manufacturing facility that uses materials processed by another department of the organisation, or an organisation's sales department that makes use of materials furnished by the organisation's marketing communications team.

Essentially, a customer is anyone who consumes anything produced or delivered by your organisation. This will include people who don't necessarily pay for the service, such as people who are service users of a public sector organisation. When defining customers, the question of who is paying for the product or service is less important than the question of who is consuming or using that product or service.

TIP 1

Make customers the agenda of your organisation – don't just put them *on* the agenda!

It's too easy for organisations to pay lip-service to the notion that their customers should be at the centre of their attentions. It's much harder for organisations to put that philosophy into practice.

Understanding and empathising wholeheartedly with your customers' agenda requires a significant imaginative effort and often an emotional investment too. How much easier it is to focus on your own agenda, your own preoccupations!

Research carried out by the consultancy Charteris suggests that most organisations devote about 70 per cent of their time and energy to their own internal preoccupations and only about 30 per cent to adding value for customers.

In fact, the ratio should, ideally, be numerically *exactly the opposite*. If you're not devoting at least 70 per cent of your time and effort to adding value for your customers, the chances are you're not impressing your customers much and also jeopardising your market share.

Customer-centricity isn't only for an organisation's most valuable customers, nor is it only the organisation's products and services that need to be aligned to customers' wants and needs. The whole *culture* of the organisation must be aligned with customers, too. Indeed, it's only when this cultural alignment has taken place that the organisation has any chance of being customer-centric.

Also, it's not just the organisation's long-term profitability that will be enhanced by taking a customer-centric approach; short-term profitability matters too.

This is another way of saying that if you make your organisation more customer-centric *now*, the benefits for you kick in right away!

And do remember: customer-centricity is dispensed by *people* in a personal sense rather than by organisations in an abstract, impersonal way.

If an organisation doesn't manage to achieve, practise and express at a grass-roots level the philosophy of customer-centricity, any attempt by an organisation to make itself customer-centric is likely to fail.

You can't be customer-centric if you don't sincerely care about your customers' agenda, and you can't be customer-centric if *you only care about your customers insofar as they are likely to buy some specific product or service you are trying to sell them.*

Instead, you need to care about your customers and their agenda in a broader, all-round sense, and I don't mean because you are trying to cross-sell to them!

Caring about customers in this broader all-round sense means understanding, among other things, how what you are trying to sell them fits into their lives, and the patterns of satisfactions they seek from those lives.

The truth is that customer-centricity is a management strategy whose time has finally come and which is now regarded as *the* business strategy for ensuring maximum wooing and retention of customers.

TIP 2

Be agile!

If you want your organisation to offer true customer-centricity to your customers, you need to make it agile — that is, you need to structure and run your organisation so that it is *rapidly responsive* to changes in what your customers want to buy from you.

Your organisation should be responding to what your customers want from you, and not vice versa.

TIP 3

Try to find a point of emotional contact between your product or service and your customers!

Associated tips:

1. Make sure you understand the meanings your customers attach to the products and services they buy from you!
2. Make sure you understand that these meanings your customers attach to the products and services they buy from you often have sensory triggers!

How can you expect to offer true customer-centricity to your customers unless they care about your product or service *emotionally*?

Ideally, you need to offer your customers something that will excite them and even turn them on, not in the sexual sense but in the sense of really getting excited by what you are offering.

I admit that inspiring excitement in a customer for your product or service is easier if you are selling something relating to leisure time – such as a book, a film, a record or some food or drink product, but there are also abundant opportunities to create excitement in business-to-business products or services.

What's the secret of creating excitement in customers? I'd say it's all about *knowing your customers well enough to know what is likely to excite them! In other words, if you want to turn your customers on, you need to know not only what buttons to press, but also why those particular buttons work.*

Another vital arrow in your quiver if you want to turn your customers on is to have a good basic understanding of the psychology behind their choices.

The first thing to bear in mind is that psychological gratification is the prime benefit of many products and services.

It follows that the more you know about these psychological gratifications, the more successful you are likely to be in selling products and services to customers.

Once you understand what your customers truly get from you, you can take steps to embody that knowledge successfully in marketing and advertising.

Many organisations already do this successfully, though there is always more that can be done, the more you know about your customers. The canniest organisations undertake quality thinking and customer research *before* a new product is launched, in order to maximise the success of that launch.

The market research industry, especially those concerned with fast-moving consumer goods – the brands you buy from supermarkets – conduct extensive research and make detailed recommendations based on the research, to help brand-owners refine ways of selling and marketing products already on the market.

For example, a UK-based market research agency, MMR Research Worldwide, is a pioneer in researching the emotional appeal to customers of the *sensory signatures* of products. The importance of this work is reflected in MMR's considerable success in the UK and its opening of overseas offices, including in the United States and China.

David Thomson, founder and chairman of MMR Research Worldwide, has been a consumer psychologist since the 1970s. He also holds the honorary title of Visiting Professor in the Department of Food and Nutritional Sciences at the University of Reading. I am grateful to Professor Thomson for the following thinking on consumer choice and sensory signatures. David has a deep understanding of why we select and buy things, and these decisions apply to *everything* we choose, including romantic partners (which I refer to as 'mates' below)!

What excites me about David's thinking is the emphasis he places on the *meaning* of what we choose. These meanings vary dramatically between people, which is why, when it comes to selecting mates, there is a vast array of different qualities that we find attractive. This is just as well, because if men and women only liked, say, women and men who look like Hollywood movie stars, the vast majority of people would never find mates and the human race would die out.

So why the variety in what we find attractive when we choose mates? Because, Professor Thomson would (I think) say: *we attach different meanings to different characteristics, and choose people with characteristics that we associate with the prospect of obtaining pleasure.*

For example, a woman who likes men who wear glasses might associate them with the nurturing her spectacle–wearing father provided for her, and so thinks that if she chooses a boyfriend who wears spectacles, she will enjoy the pleasure of being nurtured again.

Similarly, a man who likes women who are feisty and give as good as they get, might associate that characteristic with past sexual pleasure, and so will choose a feisty woman in the hope of enjoying such pleasure again.

In effect, the spectacles the man is wearing or the feistiness of a woman could be physical sensory signatures triggering the anticipation of nurturing or pleasure, to certain people.

According to Professor Thomson's thinking, when it comes to choosing different products or services rather than mates, *sensory signatures* are an aspect of a product or service that bring pleasure via one or more of our senses.

For example, if you like freshly-roasted chicken, the sight and smell of the chicken just out of the oven will be complemented by the sizzle of the pan juices in the baking tray and the anticipated taste. There might even be a touch sensation too, if you take the hot drumstick in your hand to eat it.

Commercial food and drink brands provide sensory pleasure too, often in a consciously – though by no means *cynically* – engineered way. The taste and smell of a particular food or drink brand will be complemented by the sight of its familiar package.

Touch might be involved too, as in the cool, smooth feel of a particular chocolate bar. As for the sense of hearing, it's true that this is less often involved with food or drink brands than other senses, but it can be a factor. An example would be the 'snap, crackle and pop' of Rice Krispies when milk is poured over them.

The precise impact of a sensory signature will depend on:

- its fundamental nature
- its quality
- its duration
- its magnitude
- the extent to which it is liked
- the manner in which it is *conceptualised.*

This notion of *conceptualisation* is vital to how Professor Thomson sees sensory signatures. His thinking requires its own terminology, and he draws a clear distinction between:

- what a sensory signature *is,* which he calls *perception*
- what a sensory signature *means,* which he calls *conceptualisation.*

Understanding what a sensory signature means to the individual consumer is something that Professor Thomson's organisation investigates in its research.

Essentially, a particular sensory signature will not only bring pleasure via one or more senses, but will also produce some degree of emotional satisfaction. This emotional satisfaction will not be produced in every consumer, but if emotional satisfaction is produced in enough consumers – in the sense that it is possible through research to understand and analyse the nature of the emotional satisfaction in question – that emotional satisfaction will, clearly, be of great importance in how a particular product is marketed.

In Professor Thomson's thinking and terminology, emotional satisfaction is a result of how a particular perception is conceptualised, given that we are using the word 'perception' here in the specialised meaning of what a particular sensory signature is.

Consider the well-known brand of the yeast extract Marmite. Its taste is, in Professor Thomson's terminology, a perception that leads to a conceptualisation which will in turn result in emotional satisfaction.

For example, some consumers may find that they conceptualise the taste of Marmite in a way that brings them the emotional satisfaction of thinking back to their childhoods and snug teatimes with brothers and sisters in the company of their mother.

If research were to show that this is a sufficiently widespread source of emotional satisfaction resulting from the taste of Marmite, an effort might be made to promote this comfortable childhood association in advertising and marketing.

Ideally, a brand-owner prefers that a particular emotional satisfaction resulting from a particular sensory signature will:

- be associated only with that one brand
- be something consumers like and want to experience repeatedly, and so they buy the brand again and again.

When the appeal of a sensory signature has been established among consumers, brand-owners quite rightly try hard to standardise the brand in order to ensure that customers enjoy the same gratification every time they buy it.

There is always a risk that if the brand-owner changes the nature of the product or service, even minimally, the sensory signature may no longer be delivered and customers will cease to be loyal to the brand.

A classic example of this occurred in April 1985, when the Coca-Cola Company, amidst much publicity, changed the formula to give the drink a new flavour, a new sensory signature and (crucially) a new conceptual profile.

Even if people had liked the new flavour more than the old one, the change in conceptual profile detracted hugely from their total experience and led to reduced emotional satisfaction when drinking Coke.

Perhaps for this very reason, the new flavour, New Coke, was disastrously unpopular with customers, and in the face of global complaints, within a few months Coca-Cola relaunched the old, familiar, much-loved drink, calling it 'Classic Cola'.

Classic Cola is again by far the most popular version of the drink. New Coke was discontinued as a major product by Coca-Cola, though it is still produced by some semi-independent bottlers and is popular in a few niche markets, including, reportedly, the territory of American Samoa. So if you like New Coke, you can go there to enjoy it!

This example of a drinks manufacturer getting it wrong is a dramatic illustration of food and drink brands lending themselves to having sensory signatures built into them, simply because our senses of taste and smell are closely bound up with our strongest sensuous pleasures.

An example of a non-food sensory signature that relates to hearing is the quiet purr of the Rolls-Royce's engine one hears when one is inside the car. In the past, this sensory signature featured heavily in advertisements for Rolls-

Royce cars, largely at the suggestions of advertising guru David Ogilvy, whose organisation handled the advertising for Rolls-Royce. Ogilvy was a great believer in ads communicating interesting information about products and services.

Many sensory signatures are visual. The bright scarlet colour of a can of Coca-Cola and the purple of a Cadbury's chocolate wrapper are just two examples of sensory signatures that have successfully wooed customers over several decades.

As Professor Thomson explains:

Today, new ways of understanding how consumers feel about brands are giving brand-owners unprecedented insight into what's happening at an emotional level when consumers make buying decisions. Armed with this knowledge, brand-owners have exciting opportunities to engineer emotions into their brands and enjoy global success.

Up until now, many brand-owners haven't always appreciated that when packaged goods are being sold to consumers, the product itself – not only the branding, packaging or manner in which the product is promoted – has an inherent emotional impact on the people who buy it. This explains why so many product launches and relaunches fail.

*Instead of focusing on these vitally important emotional factors, too many brand-owners ask their market research teams simply to investigate **liking** and **propensity-to-buy**. But in truth neither is an effective predictor of whether consumers are going to buy a product, let alone an indication of whether they'll make* *it part of their regular weekly shopping.*

The fact is, consumers like a lot of things they don't buy and buy a lot of things they don't like. This suggests that consumer behaviour is being guided by factors other than mere liking. But if that's so, what factors are consumers really being influenced by, and how can we measure these factors?

Having laid out his philosophy of why consumers buy what they buy, Professor Thomson elaborates as outlined below on his approach to perception and conceptualisation – concepts I have already outlined above.

My own thinking on consumer psychology is that traditional market research tests, which try to investigate liking and propensity to buy, fail to produce an adequate overview of the *real* reasons why consumers buy things.

The reason for this, in my view, is that it is all very well knowing whether or not someone *likes* something, but mere liking may not be enough for someone actually to part with their money to *buy* it, because they lack the motivation and desire to do so.

Professor Thomson believes that people buy things for the same reasons they do other things in their lives: *because they get a reward.* He calls this reward *positivity.* He also has a terminology for the experience of heightened positivity. This he calls a 'spike' of positivity.

Heightened positivity may come about as a result of special events in our lives such as holidays, falling in love, getting married, and also as a consequence of more day-to-day events: a good lunch or an excellent cup of coffee.

In practice, most of the time people are content to enjoy a stream of little spikes of positivity in their lives. Indeed, it's very likely this is the way we have evolved to enjoy life.

Many spikes of positivity are, of course, unrelated to the choice of a branded product or service. Nevertheless, brand-owners should take every reasonable step to ensure that their brand becomes intimately associated with spikes of positivity wherever possible. Doing this makes hard commercial sense. Consumers will stop buying a brand if, for some reason, it ceases bringing positivity into their lives. But brand-owners should not only be on the lookout for this. They also need to know exactly *what* their brand means to consumers and *why* their brand means what it does.

Yes, it's true that brand-owners have for a long time set their brands in a promotional context which communicates the positivity that using the brand will bring. Car ads, for example, don't just show a shiny new car in the showroom; the ad will typically depict the car in some picturesque or exotic location that is unlikely to bear much resemblance to the M25 on a dark, wet Friday evening.

Another example would be Gillette razors, which show a male model enjoying a particularly close and wonderful shave. Gillette's ambitious strapline – *the best a man can get* – is designed to make you forget that the razors are basically no more than ingeniously engineered small pieces of metal and plastic.

But even though brand-owners have often sensed intuitively the need to promote their brand in a context of positivity, they can now use exactly the same principle as a basis for a more structured approach towards *all* their marketing activity.

In particular, what should their market research really be doing? Nothing less than helping brand-owners identify and optimise the *triggers* that give consumers a heightened sense of positivity through their emotional experience of the brand.

By focusing specifically on emotional factors, a brand-owner can create a compelling point of difference between his own brand and its competitors.

What exactly are these triggers?

This brings us to the vital matter of what Professor Thomson called the product's *sensory characteristics.*

The way he sees it, what we experience when we interact with an object in the physical world is channelled to the mind via our senses. Brand-owners need to engineer deliberately-crafted associations between sensory characteristics and brand identity into their brand. These associations are what he calls sensory signatures. Brand-owners can do this by taking advantage of their understanding of how consumers see the brand.

Red Bull is a successful example of this. Even people who love Red Bull would probably agree that it is not one of the most pleasant-tasting soft drinks, yet its unusual and quirky flavour has successfully distinguished it from other carbonates, which often have adolescent or juvenile connotations.

Professor Thomson calls the process of experiencing the sensory characteristics of different stimuli *perception*. Yet perception is only part of the story, because what matters most of all, and what amounts to unlocking the mystery of consumer choice, is *the meaning consumers attach to the sensory signatures they perceive.*

Professor Thomson calls this process of attaching meaning to perception *conceptualisation.*

He argues that conceptualisation matters precisely

because buying behaviours *don't* only arise from perception, but also from how we conceptualise what we perceive. In other words, *we make a buying choice because of what the sensory signatures mean to us.*

How does conceptualisation work in practice? In the case of Red Bull, the drink's edginess, associations with extreme sports and its promise to 'vitalise body and mind' and 'give you wings', is adult and aspirational. The associated functional, emotional and other more abstract conceptualisations created by Red Bull's branding are then delivered by the drink. This is achieved in part via the physiologically and psychologically active compounds in the liquid, but also via the associations that have developed between the drink's distinctive sensory characteristics and consumers' conceptualisations of the brand.

Any competent drinks company could copy the Red Bull liquid in most respects. However, the associations that have developed between the brand-generated conceptualisations and the drink's sensory characteristics are uniquely owned by Red Bull and no other brand. 'Me too' energy drink brands do not enjoy the enormous customer mandate that Red Bull enjoys.

The importance of conceptualisation in consumer choice is huge. Armed with an understanding of it, brand-owners can create market research programmes designed to give them a detailed understanding of precisely what kind of emotional meanings consumers attach to their products through conceptualisation.

Professor Thomson's organisation MMR Research Worldwide has developed a philosophy of branding based around a matrix that plots three aspects of a brand – *branding* (we take this to mean how a brand-owner communicates, promotes and advertises their branded offer), *product,* and *packaging* – against the three criteria of how the whole branded offer is conceptualised by consumers. The three criteria are:

- *Liking*: this refers to the immediate enjoyment yielded by the product experience.

- *Emotionality*: this refers to the emotional conceptualisations conveyed by the product.

- *Functionality*: this refers to the functional conceptualisations conveyed. For example, does a new energy drink *taste like* it will keep you awake with the ability to dance all night? This might well be different from the *actual*, scientifically-provable power the drink has to give energy to customers.

As Professor Thomson explains:

Applying market research to the task of investigating what a brand means emotionally to consumers brings scientifically sound, quantitative research to an area often dominated by qualitative research. Brand-owners can now use these research techniques to get access to brand and product profiles that reveal all the associated emotions and conceptualisations – putting a measure on every one.

For a brand-owner, the secret of success is to make the product a response to what the research has uncovered, and to optimise all elements of the branded offer (such as the formulation or product design, packaging, marketing and promotion) so that they are conceptually harmonious in order to maximise their potential emotional appeal to consumers, whenever and wherever they encounter the brand.

Professor Thomson's fascinating and in-depth thinking essentially aims to exploit – and not in any cynical fashion, either – a particular aspect of human psychology for the purposes of making consumer products not only attractive to customers but – and this is, I think, a major point – part of customers' own emotional experience and enjoyment of life.

Who is to say that doing this is not an important service to humanity? Who is to say that a teenager may not get as much of a buzz from drinking Red Bull with his or her friends as an opera buff gets from watching a great performance of *Madame Butterfly*? As apostles of customer-centricity, it is not our job to make judgements about what people want. Instead, our job is to find out *what* they want and, if our business involves meeting that need, to meet it to the very best of our abilities.

When we look at Professor Thomson's philosophy of customer desire, we can see that his approach is an extrapolation of the basic principle that *organisations need to take every step to understand what their customers are really getting from them.*

Which brings me back to the very first point I mentioned in this tip.

TIP 4

Know the five questions your customers will have in their minds when deciding if you are making them happy!

This tip is all about making customer-centricity work in practice.

As a matter of common sense, any activity directed around maximising an organisation's customer-centricity must start with an assessment of how customer-centric the organisation is at that moment.

This initial assessment needs to look in particular detail at the following five questions, which should be considered from the customer's perspective.

Is your organisation making it easy for me to deal with you?

Does your organisation give me an enjoyable experience when I deal with you?

Does your organisation understand me?

Does your organisation continually improve my

experience as a customer?

Does your organisation present me with products and services that delight me?

The extent to which your organisation is answering these questions with a 'yes' is an indication of how happy you are likely to be making your customers feel.

This tip leads on to other tips that stem from these five questions, as follows. . .

TIP 5

Make it easy for your customers to deal with you!

The secret of helping your customers deal with you so that the entire process becomes a doddle is always the same: *look at things through their eyes.*

If you follow this rule, you can't go wrong, because after all, the whole essence of customer-centricity is to listen to customers and to give them what they want.

Never assume that just because your organisation has been dealing with customers in a certain way for a long time, your customers will want to continue with you in that way for the rest of eternity. They won't. What they want is to be able to deal with your organisation as effortlessly as possible and to get the products and services they really need from you.

Too much is spoken about multi-channel, as if it were some Open Sesame to the perfect customer relationship. But the truth is that what customers want isn't actually multi-channel, but the biggest choice of channels relevant to their particular needs.

For some customers, this means just one channel: they want to visit a retail outlet and pay cash for something they want to buy. If you install an internet-driven automated sales machine in the store which requires them to use their debit card, and they don't want to use their debit card, you're not helping them. I know that such internet-drive devices are important because they allow your customers to access your entire range of products and services when you aren't able to keep everything in stock. But give customers what they want: why force them to pay by card when they don't want to? It's irrelevant that debit cards are easier for you: you're not in business to make things easier for you; you're in business to make things easier for your customers!

Give customers the ease of access they want; find out what they really want and *how* they want to buy from you.

Gear yourself up to what your customers want. Conversely, there's no need to *over-service* your customers, if it's not what they want. For instance, many organisations can order in a product for the following day for a customer who wanted it when it was not in stock. However, maybe your customer does not need the product the following day; next week will do just as well. If you order it in for them the following day and they don't want that, all you're doing is usiing resources to doing something that could be used better elsewhere.

Too many organisations set an initial key performance indicator (KPI) which matters to them rather than their customers. The classic example is call centres, which effectively give their operatives a time limit on how long a call should take, and if the goal of the call (from the organisation's point of view) is not met in that time, they will want the call ended. However, a KPI should be based on what customers want, rather than what the organisation wants.

TIP 6

Show your customers that you truly understand them!

As always, the golden rule is to *listen to customers*.

Customers will talk to you every day and in every way, if you take the trouble to listen to them. They will tell you what they buy from you and why and when and how they buy it. They might even tell you more than you need to know: although you'll need to get used to the idea that you do need to know more from your customers than you might have thought you did in the past.

We are at the start of a revolution in 'customer voice' which I am sure will run for hundreds of years. Social networks are making it easy for organisations to listen to the voice of an individual. Customers will make complaints on Twitter and Facebook and other social networks, and organisations can usually programme their computer systems to take note of those comments and to make remarks on-line that deal with the complaint.

This is not just about agreeing with everything customers

say: there will be times when it is simply not practical for you to do whatever the customer wants. There might be, for example, cost reasons why the customer cannot have everything they want. However, the fact that you have paid attention to their needs means that they will respect you for doing this.

I realise that the business of detecting on-line remarks about your organisation is a complex one, and that sometimes you will not be able to do it because the conversation is taking place privately. But realistically, most conversations on social networks are in the public domain and if they are, it is perfectly legitimate for you to listen in and make helpful comments.

Remember that most customers are not overly sophisticated in what they want from you. They just want products that do what they expect – and ideally, go beyond their expectation.

TIP 7

Make sure you continually improve your customers' experience!

In business, as in life, treading water doesn't work for long. Your customers don't just want a great experience now, they want an experience that gets better, ideally all the time.

I suppose we like novelty and we want things to get better all the time. After all, you wouldn't be very happy in a personal relationship that didn't get better all the time, would you?

How can you make your customers' experience improve continually? You can achieve this by doing any of the following, and ideally, all of them:

- *keep making your products and services better.* This is something you should be doing as a matter of course. It's easier to do if you know what you are *really* selling to your customers – that is, if you know what the real value-added benefit is that they get when they buy from you. This is discussed in **Tip Number 11.**

- *keep making the quality of the service you offer better.*
One of the biggest challenges facing an organisation,
whatever its size, is how best to look after the needs
of thousands or even millions of customers while
improving customer service all the time. This is less of
a problem for smaller businesses, as they are likely to
know all their customers personally, but as a business
grows, it is all too easy for it to treat its customers
more like numbers than people (or worse, sums of
money it can make from them). Ultimately, the only
way to avoid this problem is to *want* to avoid it. Good
customer-facing technology can help. For example, if
you are delivering a lot of your customer service via
a call centre, technology that enables call centre staff
to view personal notes about customers the moment
the customer's call is taken, will enable staff to give
personal attention to them from the word go.

- *recruit staff who love working with customers.*
Customer-centricity is delivered by people, not
by organisations. The key to continuous service
improvement can only be found in hiring staff who
actively enjoy looking after customers. Waitrose, the
retail food chain that is part of John Lewis, is very
good at this. When you're shopping in Waitrose and
want to find where something is, the staff are trained
to take you to the appropriate aisle rather than just
telling you which one it is. They are also trained to
ask after they've escorted you to where you want
to be, whether there's anything else they can help

you with. What I love about Waitrose staff is their sincerity; when they ask you if there's anything else they can do to help they really sound as if they mean it! For more on recruiting the right kind of staff, see **Tip Number 14**.

- *look hard at your customer service delivery channels.* Think hard how you can improve the way service is delivered to customers. This isn't only a question of using state-of-the-art technology; it's also a matter of applying customer-focused thinking to what will most benefit the customer, and basing your customer service delivery plans on delivering those benefits. **As always, with any customer-centric business strategy, the essence of success is taking the time, trouble and imaginative effort to see things from the customer's point of view.**

Overall, never forget that you can only keep on improving the products and services you offer your customers if you know enough about them and what they want from you.

Always, always, always look at things through customers' eyes. You need to create an *environment, structure,* and *mindset* within your organisation, dedicating all three elements to your customers' interests.

Commit yourself to looking after your customers on a long-term basis. Seek long-term relationships with them. A customer is for life, not just for Christmas!

TIP 8

Offer your customers products and services that delight them!

The secret of offering your customers products and services that delight them is to know enough about your customers to know what they want.

The movie *The Social Network* (2010), apart from being an entertaining film about how Facebook was founded, is also illuminating from a customer-centricity perspective. Mark Zuckerberg, Facebook's founder, is portrayed as a young man who is not too adept at dealing emotionally with the world (especially not with young women). But there's no doubt that he has an instinctive feeling for what customer-centricity is.

Early on in the film he grasps the basic principle of Facebook – that it gives people a computer-based, virtual version of the social experience of being at college. One of the many delights of the film is that it dramatises the rapid responsiveness of Mark and his colleagues to what their customers want. This forms the very basis of the Facebook concept: that access to the information on a user's 'wall' – that is, their own particular page – is limited to their friends rather than open to all and sundry.

There's also a scene in which one of Mark's college acquaintances asks him if he knows whether a particular girl is in a relationship or not. This question inspires Mark to invent the Facebook feature that many people find especially interesting: the Relationship Status feature. Whatever you think of this feature, you can't deny that its presence on Facebook is an obvious example of Facebook's desire to practise customer-centricity.

In practical terms within the business world there are basically three classes of products and services.

The first is where the product or service meets a fundamental need. Examples of this are most fast-moving consumer goods, including food and drink products.

The second is where it offers customers aspirational delight. This means that customers derive a benefit from it that exceeds the limited benefit they would get from a fundamental need being satisfied. Naturally, advertisers try hard to transform a product supplying a basic need into one that offers aspirational delight: you could argue that almost all advertising aims to do precisely that.

Not all products or services that meet a fundamental need can be boosted into providing aspirational delight. For example, your local council's emptying of your dustbins is a fundamental need that's hard to glamorise. Similarly, dishcloths cannot readily be boosted into anything aspirational.

But this isn't true, for example, of toilet paper, which comes in many different brands designed to offer benefits of softness, thickness and so on, adding up to more than just a basic product. Detergents such as washing-up liquid, detergent for dishwashers and laundry powders and liquids are designed and advertised in the most astonishing ways to extol their cleaning powers and the benefits of sparkling, fragrantly clean clothes and wonderfully clean pots, pans, cutlery and glasses from the dishwasher.

Dishwasher detergent is a case in point. The whole idea of designing dishwasher detergents in the form of small, potent tablets is essentially a marketing ploy, when a simple liquid, while equally effective, might not be so easy to brand and market. And is it just me, or is there not extraordinary ingenuity devoted to the physical appearance of the tablets? They are produced in a variety of colours to symbolise the variety of functions they offer. Some are even designed with a red ball in the middle that provides a visual sense of the different potencies in the tablet. I sometimes wonder whether the red ball and its appearance has a vaguely erotic or sensuous role. In any event, many customers swear by premium brand dishwasher tablets, when there is ample evidence that basic ones do the job just as well, especially if you're in an area where water is relatively soft. And if you're not, it is much cheaper to put water-softening salt into the dishwasher than to spend a lot of money on more ornate tablets.

Yet manufacturers of the more ornate tablets know just what they are doing.

The third class of products and services is very different from the first two, in that it *meets a need that the customer didn't even know he or she had*!

This is a common class of technology products. Here, the customer is presented with a product they didn't know existed or only half-imagined might exist. We might call it 'the Apple effect', in tribute to the remarkable range of consumer electronic devices that Apple have brought to the world over the past decade.

If you want to maximise your success, you need ideally to inject some aspirational delight into your products. You want to move them from the class of meeting a fundamental need into the class of offering delight.

I mentioned Gillette razors above, but it's useful to emphasise here that they are designed to provide a close shave rather than to make men who use them feel like James Bond. In practice, the advertising tends to combine both benefits: it emphasises the close shave, but doesn't baulk at conveying the idea that Gillette razors make their users into a very special kind of man. Whatever you think of this approach to advertising razors, it appears to work, mainly because Gillette has a good understanding of what its customers want from it.

TIP 9

Find out who your customers really are!

In the past, it was no doubt much easier for people who were selling things to know who their customers were. If you'd been running a bazaar stall in Ancient Egypt, for example, your customers would simply have been the people who came along to buy things. That's still true today of most retail businesses; the basic business model is much the same today as it's always been.

But in many other businesses, and especially businesses that feature relatively complex supply chains, it is often difficult to be sure who the end-user customer actually is.

Take book publishing. On the face of it, when a publisher publishes a book, the customer is the person who will buy the book. This itself creates some complexity, because people who buy books are not necessarily those for whom the book is intended.

This applies, for example, to books for children and indeed to most gifts for children, such as toys. In the book publishing world, publishers tend to spend as much time and energy (if not money) on promoting to bookshops as to consumers. Some advertisements for books are directed at consumers, but they tend to be restricted to print media and – curiously (at least in the UK) – to railway station posters. But most marketing of books by publishers is directed at bookshop managers. It is true that Amazon as a bookseller has changed the dynamic to some extent, since Amazon makes use of readers' reviews to market books. But even so, for most publishers, the major customer tends to be bookshop managers who will make vital decisions about which books they want to stock. Some retailers only take books that are already successful. This particularly applies to supermarkets and, in the UK, to the retailer W.H. Smith.

The pharmaceutical industry is another example of an industry where the end-user is not necessarily who we think it is.

In the case of over-the-counter drugs that can be bought without a prescription, the consumer is the obvious customer, and a great deal of marketing is directed at consumers. However, in the case of prescription drugs, the end-user is not the decision-maker – the patient's doctor is the decision-maker, and drug companies devote great energy to persuading doctors to prescribe certain drugs for their patients. Drug company representatives regularly visit doctors, and advertisements for prescription drugs frequently appear in the specialised medical press that is read almost entirely by the medical community.

On the face of it, working out who your customer really is, for a particular product or service, simply requires intelligence and an understanding of your supply chain. It is often the case that people who recommend products and services to end-user customers are not accorded the status they deserve by organisations selling the products or services in question. You should always be mindful of who these advisers are. They deserve serious attention in any marketing activity you are undertaking.

Much of my work on customer-centricity projects is carried out in the public sector, where very often the end-user is not paying for the product or service at all, or is only doing so because they are a tax-payer. In public sector projects, it is easy for a large organisation such as a healthcare trust to forget that the people to whom services are being provided – such as adult healthcare services – are customers, even though they are not paying for the services themselves. This is a risky mentality, because once you forget that a particular user is a customer, the next step is relative indifference to the interests of the user. It is fair to say that this relative indifference has often prevented public sector service delivery being as efficient as it could.

A major problem in the UK is that healthcare organisations do not share information with each other in the way they could if they were to offer maximum customer-centricity to their patients.

For example, Mrs Smith, aged 78, falls over at home and badly bruises her right leg. She is in a lot of pain and calls an ambulance that takes her to the local hospital. But even after a week, when the bruising subsides, she is kept in the hospital for a further week because she isn't very mobile. Only after those two weeks does a social worker who knows Mrs Smith hear what has happened to her, and she hurries to the hospital. There, the social worker explains to the hospital staff that Mrs Smith has never been too mobile anyway, but has always been perfectly happy at home with friends and relatives visiting her and regular help from social services. The social worker then takes Mrs

Smith home, but Mrs Smith's unnecessary extra week in hospital has given her bedsores and made her less mobile now than she was before. She takes a long time to recover.

This kind of scenario isn't a fantasy but is played out thousands of times every day in the UK today. It's caused by different healthcare providers not having centralised access to the same information about particular patients. The lack of this information costs the NHS tens of millions of pounds every day in unnecessary hospital stays and other inefficiencies in the care system.

The consequences of this lack of information-sharing by inter-providers can sometimes have disastrous consequences if crucial patient information is not readily available at the right time.

A dream in the healthcare profession – a dream for patients, anyway – is that every entity they interact with, whether a GP practice, hospital, ambulance service, social care department or any other provider of healthcare, has instant access to a computer system that integrates all the information gathered about a patient into a single source of reference. Different providers would be able to access this at will.

I very much hope that the question of UK healthcare entities collaborating more efficiently will be solved in the future, and I am confident that it will be. But the fact that it is a problem at all is, I think, because it has often been difficult for healthcare professionals to think of patients as the customers that they truly are.

Indeed, some UK healthcare organisations have addressed the patient / customer problem by giving patients a new level of control, effectually allocating to them a personal budget for the services they are given during the year and enabling them to make their own decisions about what services to 'buy' with their allocated money.

TIP 10

Find out what your customers really want from you!

Barbara Lammers is a resourceful woman who both enjoys and creates art. When she was bringing up her two sons in Antigua, she used to supplement the family income by making decorative papier mâché fridge magnets bearing Antiguan designs and the name of the island. These were popular with tourists.

Some years later, Barbara moved back to Britain. She started working for a computer services company but this didn't work out, so she looked round for something else to do.

Then a friend, who ran a business in the Netherlands selling mosaic tiles, suggested Barbara might want to start selling the tiles in the UK. Barbara started up her business, Mosaic Trader UK, from her front room. Nowadays she employs three people, working from a large warehouse on the outskirts of Canterbury in Kent. Her business is successful and growing. As she says:

I never see what I do as just selling mosaic tiles and the other things that people need to make mosaics. Those are my products, yes, but what I'm really selling are things that give people a great time and let them relax and be creative in a way that many of them have never experienced before. Some of my customers are professional mosaic artists; others are amateurs who love making mosaics. My customers also include health service organisations whose patients find making mosaics therapeutic.

Barbara's enthusiasm for what she does is infectious. She is customer-centric precisely because she understands instinctively and completely that what she is really selling is not mosaic tiles so much as opportunities for her customers to become creative, artistic and absorbed in a satisfying pastime. Making mosaics takes its devotees into a world far removed from the stresses of modern life. As Barbara puts it:

Mosaics have been created for at least 5,000 years. Nowadays superb and beautiful results can be achieved in a short time-frame even by people who don't have any artistic experience. The modern mosaic artist's colour palette is wonderfully varied.

In other words, the inherent beauty of the materials does some of the artistic work for you. Even beginners can create beautiful results within a few hours.

Barbara Lammers believes wholeheartedly in what she sells and in the delight her products bring to her customers. She knows, crucially, *why* her customers buy from her and what she is really selling to them. Her warehouse during working hours always has a buzz of customer-centric activity about it. The affectionate care she and her colleagues take in packing the products up before they go off to customers by post, courier or shipping says a great deal about why Barbara is such a disciple of customer-centricity . . . and why her business is doing so well.

Mark McCormack's *What they don't teach you at Harvard Business School* contains many great anecdotes. One of the best concerns a conversation McCormack once had with one of his clients, André Heiniger, then the chairman of Rolex. McCormack relates that he once asked Heiniger how things were going in the watch business.

'I really haven't the faintest idea,' Heiniger replied.

McCormack, astonished that the chairman of one of the most famous watch manufacturers in the world could possibly respond like this, asked Heiniger what he meant.

'Rolex is not in the watch business,' Heiniger said. 'Rolex is in the *luxury* business.'

This tells us everything we ought to bear in mind when thinking about the enormously important matter of what our customers are getting from us.

You can only keep your customers happy if you properly understand what they are getting from you.

I'm not saying that if you understand this, it means that your customers *are* getting what they want from you –this won't automatically be the case. But certainly, your only useful starting-point in managing relationships with your customers is knowing what they are getting from you right now.

Ironically, the more obvious it may seem to you that you know what you are selling, the more you need to do some hard thinking and research when working out what your customers are getting from you.

The problem is, most businesses are too busy dealing with daily business problems – fulfilling orders, trying to keep customers happy – to think about what their customers are getting from them, and some businesses get it completely wrong.

Take the example of typewriter companies. During the late nineteenth century, and for much of the twentieth century up until the 1980s, typewriter manufacture was big business. Yet the only typewriter manufacturer who not only survived the advent of word-processors but became a big player in the word-processing market was IBM, the manufacturer of the famous 'golfball' typewriter. IBM was a special case, since it only made typewriters as a sideline; its main business was making punched-card electromechanical 'tabulator' business machines which were the world's first automatic data processing devices – and, incidentally, the direct ancestor of the first electromechanical digital computer, funded by IBM and completed in 1944.

Most organisations specialising in selling typewriters failed to make the transition to word-processors because they had not fully grasped what they were selling. They thought they were selling typewriters but, in fact, what they were selling *were machines that allowed customers to create, produce and print out documents*. If typewriter manufacturers had understood this, they would have jumped at the chance to sell word-processors, which of course made it far easier to create successive copies of documents: and trust me, anyone writing a book knows how important that is. You need a good word-processor *and* a large waste-paper basket.

Ultimately, there's no shortcut to knowing the real meaning to your customers of what they are getting from you. Practical research, aimed at finding out what they think of your products and services, and the role these products and services play in their lives, is essential. Applying sheer common sense and your knowledge of human psychology and behaviour to the matter is also important.

This type of thinking can reveal some interesting, and even surprising conclusions. We have already mentioned luxury watches, and the fact that that André Heiniger of Rolex knew Rolex was in the luxury rather than the watch business. Let's now look at a few more examples of products and services where the true nature of what customers are getting from a product or service is by no means as straightforward as one might think.

Diet books

These books are (at least on the face of it) designed to help us lose weight. But the inescapable fact is that – judging from the very high sales figures of the most successful of these volumes – there are millions more people buying them than are actually losing weight. This suggests that what customers are getting out of the books is very different from mere dietary advice.

It appears that what they are getting is *the feeling of gratification that they are doing something positive about losing weight*. Only a small proportion of readers actually go on to take action and lose weight.

Of course, this is another way of saying that diet books are peddling hope.

Losing weight is hard; it involves depriving oneself to a lesser or greater extent of the pleasure of eating, and it involves feeling hungry. Being hungry makes you feel unhappy, even though after a while your stomach shrinks and you don't need as much food, you eat less and you don't feel so hungry.

All the same, dieting is hard. Buying a diet book is a pleasant way to feel you are making progress without having to suffer.

Lottery tickets

On the face of it, people buy a lottery ticket because they want to win the lottery. But as the vast majority of people don't achieve this aim, and don't expect to win, common sense suggests that what customers really get from buying a lottery ticket is *the feeling of hope that they might win.* Buyers of lottery tickets can enjoy this feeling between buying the ticket and the results of the draw being publicised.

What they are really buying is *psychological gratification*. Though this shouldn't surprise you, because, if you delve into what customers are getting from many of the things they're buying, you realise that what they are actually buying *is* psychological benefit.

Luxury watches

We have seen what the chairman of Rolex considered to be the true nature of the business he was in. But there is more to say about luxury watches: as all mobile phones nowadays show the time, there is no need for people to buy watches if they carry a mobile phone. I don't know what the proportion is, globally, of mobile phone owners who also have watches, but no doubt it is high. The watches are clearly being bought for some other reason than to tell the time; the purchase is yet another psychological gratification.

Which is, by the by, a perfectly good reason for buying it. We spend much of our lives seeking to feel good about ourselves. This is by no means an easy task. If purchasing a luxury watch (and so providing employment to the people who design and make the watch) is a short-cut to psychological gratification, fair enough.

Energy drinks

From a medical point of view, 'energy' drinks are completely unnecessary for anyone following a healthy and balanced diet. If someone needs a sudden rush of caffeine and sugar, hot sweet coffee or hot chocolate will generally do the job better than a can of cold fizzy drink.

But this simple point is of no interest to purchasers of energy drinks, who derive a whole range of psychological benefits from a purchase which is lost on people who are not fans of these drinks, much as the pleasure of listening to 'rap' music is lost on those who are not attracted to this kind of music.

The benefits that lovers of energy drinks perceive themselves as enjoying when they buy their favourite drink arise from factors relating to status, lifestyle choice and peer pressure. These perceived benefits have made energy drinks a global sales phenomenon in recent years.

The most successful energy drink of all, Red Bull, sells about three million cans a day globally. The fact that it tastes like sweetened mouthwash – without even delivering the benefits that mouthwash offers – doesn't seem to deter its fans. There is, after all, no accounting for taste, though Red Bull's accountants probably wouldn't agree.

Insurance

This is a useful and relatively rare example of a product where the prime benefit is psychological. After all, most people buying insurance *don't want* the event against which they are insuring to ever happen.

The benefit they get from the insurance policy is peace of mind in the knowledge that, should the unwanted event happen, they will receive benefits that will offset – if only partially – the impact of the event.

Summing up, to become fully customer-centric you need to understand what you are really selling to your customers. And what you are really selling them is, deep down, the *benefit* they get from what they buy from you. That benefit may not be anything like as obvious as you think it is. Indeed, if the benefit you are selling seems obvious, maybe you should look deeper and ask yourself if it's as obvious as it seems to be.

Having made sure you know what your customers are really buying from you, you need to know why your customers are buying specifically from *you*. I look at this in **Tip 16.**

TIP 11

Remember that the core of customer-centricity is adding value!

Within the world of business – a term which embraces products and services delivered by public service organisations as well as by profit-making organisations – added value is:

> the benefit, perceived by the customer, that he or she gains from a particular product or service above and beyond the intrinsic 'face value' of that product.

A useful example here is the mobile phone. On the face of it, a mobile phone is simply a piece of electronic technology. However, the mobile phone's added value, coupled with an air time agreement, is a tool that the customer can use to manage his or her life.

In a similar way, a television – on the face of it a complex piece of technology that enables broadcast images to be displayed, with synchronised sound, on a screen – offers its customers a window on the world.

You get the idea. Clearly, the more added value a product or service can offer, the more attractive that product or service will be.

Unfortunately, too many organisations, far from delivering added value, barely deliver the face value of what they purport to offer. All too often the question of whether they are delivering added value comes down less to how effective their customer service delivery systems are (though this will be a factor) than to the *personal attitude of staff*.

Helpful staff who want to assist their customers can deliver a far greater service quality than unhelpful staff, even if they are using the same customer service delivery systems. Basically, what is needed is a *discretionary effort* (which may well be above and beyond what the staff member is expected to do to fulfil the terms of his or her employment).

In practice, the majority of services we are offered by customer service staff, whether in person or via remote delivery channels, only work if the customer service people who are delivering the service truly want to help customers.

I've suggested what added value is. The question now is: what exactly is added value at a technical level? I'd say: *it is something we can see, hear, feel, smell, touch or are aware of psychologically and emotionally, and which we see as important and improving our lives.*

Even a book or film fits this definition, because while the book or film may give us enjoyable thoughts and memories (just as a piece of toast with butter and Marmite might do), the book or film itself was initially a tangible experience: something that – if our senses were working normally – we saw or heard.

When deciding whether or not a particular product or service constitutes added value, it is useful to ask three questions:

1. *Is the customer prepared to pay for and/or invest in the time or activity involved in using the product or service?*

This is a vital initial question to ask. It's important to remember that the customer may be paying for the activity without being conscious of it. For example, a 'free' helpline is of course not really free; its cost is embedded in the cost of the product or service being sold.

The question is important for many reasons, not least because there is a difference between something being an integral part of the service and the customer perceiving it as adding value. An everyday example of this is the security check that an operator in a call centre goes through with you before proceeding with the call. You might find the security check irritating, but the call cannot go on without it. However, a customer cannot be expected to regard the security check as part of the added value.

2. *Does the activity improve something from the customer's perspective?*

If it does, we can be sure that the activity will be perceived by the customer as adding value.

3. *Is the activity being completed accurately first time?*

This may seem a rather obscure question, but it is extremely important. An activity that a customer perceives as adding value if it is completed accurately *the first time* will very likely cease to be perceived as adding value if it has to be repeated.

For example, a customer who calls a helpline and then feels obliged to call the helpline again because he or she does not feel that all their questions were answered the first time round, is unlikely to regard the second call (or successive calls) as constituting added value.

These three questions can be applied in either of two ways.

Firstly, you could take the view that if the answer to any question is negative, then the activity cannot be customer-centric.

Secondly, you could use the questions more informally to assess the activity for its customer-centricity.

By the way, I don't think that we have a right to make judgements about what our customers like. If we don't approve of the things they like to buy from us, perhaps we shouldn't be selling them those products in the first place! In any case, the whole essence of customer-centricity is, at heart, empathising with customers, and we can only empathise with customers if we like what we are selling to them and believe in it.

If you don't believe in what you are selling to your customers and if you don't like selling it to them, I don't see how you can provide added value to them. This is such an important point that I think it deserves a tip of its own.

TIP 12

Choose something to sell to your customers that you *like* selling!

I'm a keen fan of science-fiction stories. I have no doubt that, if an intelligent alien species were to visit Earth, the alien would be impressed by many aspects of our planet, but perhaps particularly by the sheer multitude of things we make and sell to each other. Essentially, what we call the business world is in fact the vast infrastructure of products we make for each other and which we use mostly on the surface of the Earth, though some are deployed up to seven miles below the surface and some up to 100 miles into space, and beyond!

If you think about it, this remarkable world of ours – I mean the human world, not the natural world – is *all* built by work, and as all work is, ultimately, done for a customer, it's no exaggeration to say that selling things to customers is the basis of all human economic activity other than when people are growing and/or making things that they will eat, or use, themselves.

Even in developing countries where people need to find customers or risk starvation, people will discover that there are some occupations more congenial to them than others, and in which they will do better. Indeed, the more desperate the economic situation, the more vital – in every sense – customer-centricity is likely to be.

In a world replete with products and services that people sell to one another, doesn't it make the most profound sense for you to choose some product or service to sell – or at least to produce – that you *like* to sell, something that you are *passionate* about selling?

After all, aren't we always going to do best at delivering customer-centricity when we love what we are supplying to our customers?

TIP 13

Remember that the customer-centricity mindset should stay with you even after you leave the office!

Over the decades when I've been developing my own theories and practice in customer-centricity, I've come to believe wholeheartedly that it's extremely difficult for anyone to become truly customer-centric in their professional life if they have two distinct personae: their business/professional persona and their 'personal life' persona.

Too many business books operate on the basis that the reader has a business/professional persona (which the business books target in their tutoring activities), and also a more general persona – which the books usually ignore.

Self-help books are directed at the reader's entire personality, but most business books are aimed only at the business side of the reader's mindset.

True, there are exceptions: the late Mark McCormack's

excellent *What they don't teach you at Harvard Business School* is one. In his book – a handy collection of pithy nuggets of practical tried-and-tested business advice – he takes for granted that he is seeking not only to modify the reader's attitude to business but also the reader's whole personality.

Generally, though, business books tend to be directed at the business side of the reader's thinking and personality, as if that were something entirely distinct from the rest of that person.

This attitude makes no sense to me. Surely now, more than at any other time in history, the rigid demarcation between a person's professional / business persona and their personal persona is becoming blurred – assuming, of course, that the polarisation was ever valid in the first place, which I doubt.

There are many reasons for this blurring. These include:

The changing nature of work

Ultimately, the blurring of professional and personal roles arises from the changing nature of work itself.

The time was, when after leaving school or further education, people got a job with a particular organisation or sector, and tended to stay there most or all of their lives. True, the idea of a job for life was always a bit of a fantasy – jobs have always been precarious – but nevertheless, in the past, people's careers tended to be focused around specific organisations or sectors.

To some extent this remains true today, but for more and more people, jobs tend to be increasingly *project-based*.

Typically, you're hired to undertake a specific project or sets of projects, and your performance determines whether you continue to be employed on that project or whether you are given other projects.

This trend has gone along with – and has been furthered by – burgeoning competition in most sectors, including cross-border *and* cross-sector competition. Much less is sacred in professional life today than was the case in the past. Hand in hand with this secularisation is the increasing informality of manner and dress in business and professional life.

Today, in business everything is up for grabs. Foreign ownership of renowned domestic brands? It's as commonplace as foreign ownership of major domestic utilities suppliers. Wars have been fought in the past to stop major national assets from passing into foreign ownership, but in recent years the chequebook has often won over what tanks, airplanes and infantry regiments could not.

Competition and hunger for success means that, today, there are few crevices within the private, for-profit sector where employees can languish comfortably by staying uncontroversial, not causing trouble, and doing as little as possible to keep their jobs.

Instead, *everyone* has to be on their toes and do their best to get top-level results if they want to keep on paying their mortgage.

What's true of the private sector is becoming more and more true of the public sector. The days when a job in the public sector was a job for life will soon have vanished completely.

The reason for the increasing lack of indolent bolt-holes in the public sector is that governments nowadays, not unreasonably, feel that tax-payers' hard-won money needs to be spent just as efficiently as private capital. More so, indeed, for doesn't every government have an elected and moral responsibility to give tax-payers the very best value for money?

Indeed, I'm glad this is the case, for over the past few years my main professional activity has been working with local councils in Britain to transform the way they look after the people they were created to serve.

More and more people see their professional life as a matter of successfully carrying out specific projects, in the same way that an actor or writer sees their career as a succession of hard-won acting or writing credits.

More and more evidence of a project-based approach to careers can be seen even in very large organisations. People's careers tend increasingly to be based not on 'working for' the organisation, but on performing specific projects within the organisation. And, as in so many areas of professional life, you're only regarded as being as good as your last project.

There's a flipside to this. Few people have much job security nowadays, and this is as much to do with the changing nature of work as with economic factors.

Today employees – and employers too – need to be on their toes all the time.

Of course, the phenomenon of increasingly project-based business life can seem unfair. Seniority counts for less than it once did, and winning a senior position in an organisation is no longer a gravy train to a prosperous life and, in due course, a fat pension. Indeed, senior people are always under ever more pressure to perform than middle-rank and junior employees.

As for chief executives, the general public, marvelling at their salaries, forgets just how short-term many of their positions actually are. Three years is, in most sectors, a pretty good innings for a chief executive: mergers, acquisitions, changes in corporate strategy, private indiscretions, physical health problems or sheer burn-out tend to conspire against professional longevity.

What does all this mean for you?

It means, by and large, that it no longer makes sense for you to hand over the responsibility for a successful career to the organisation you work for.

Instead, your career is increasingly likely to consist of a 'portfolio' of professional positions and activities, possibly including one or more spells of self-employment. It's difficult to know in advance what the nature of that portfolio will be. What *is* certain is that the factor common to all the career positions in your portfolio will be *you*. You, and your developing and broadening professional and personal skills.

And because nowadays it's going to be you who is at the heart of your own career management rather than any of the organisations you work for or with, it makes abundant sense that you should aim to develop every aspect of yourself career-wise. This means ensuring that your entire personality, mindset, and range of skills are involved in that development.

The practical fact of how people think

There's another key factor in the blurring between your professional or business persona and your personal persona. It's this: even if it were psychologically possible to present two completely different personae to the world – your 'professional life' persona and your 'personal life' persona – it would be stressful to do, and no way to live. You are one person, not two. You are who you are, and you can't escape that.

It *is* possible, when you go to work, to hang up your 'leisure life personality' in the company cloakroom and pick up a new 'work-life personality' module from your locker. But people who do this – or whose jobs require them to do this – are unlikely to achieve much, at least, not in that particular job. How can you perform your highest potential if you are not being true to yourself? How can you achieve all you are capable of, if you are only giving half of yourself? No: ideally you need a job or occupation where you can be true to yourself, and if you don't have such a job *now*, it's a fair bet that you will be restless until you find one.

The reality of how you are assessed to work on a particular project, or are interviewed for a particular new job

Any interview for a job worth having involves not just your professional skills but your entire personality being scrutinised – especially if you're competing for a project as a self-employed person, or as a consultancy.

Every aspiring consultant needs to show evidence of having the right technical skills for the potential assignment along with testimonials that demonstrate expertise. Overall, however, what wins new clients and projects for any self-employed person is their personality.

The higher you progress in your career, the more important your personality becomes compared with your technical skills

This is another reason for the increased blurring between work life and leisure life personae. The higher up you go in a corporate hierarchy, the higher you ascend in any self-employed, advisory or consultancy role, the more your entire personality matters.

This can be seen in all commercial and industrial sectors. Career progression means an emphasis on management, and management skills are always predominantly *interpersonal*.

Indeed, in most career paths a point will come where, if your personality does *not* win you promotion to management level or bring you success when you reach management level, you are likely to encounter setbacks in your career.

For example, a successful dealer in a financial institution will sooner or later be invited to lead a team of dealers. This is by no means always an easy transition, for such a dealer is likely to discover that managing a team demands substantially different skills from those required to be a lone dealer. Similarly, technical specialists in any discipline often find the transition to management difficult.

Interestingly, chief executives of large organisations like to keep their desks clear and uncluttered. Surely this demonstrates that what they see themselves offering in their professional life is their *entire personality*, rather than their skill at dealing with bits of documentation.

The very fact that the higher up an executive goes in an organisation, the less cluttered their desk tends to be, confirms, I think, that the higher up one goes, the more one's personality matters.

Increasing technological progress throughout society tends to create more jobs requiring 'personality'

If we could catapult ourselves back in time to the business world of the nineteenth century or the first thirty years of the twentieth century, we would be amazed at the high proportion of jobs requiring physical skill and effort compared with those requiring brainpower and personality.

Today, with sophisticated machines and high-tech tools performing tasks previously carried out by human beings, a greater proportion of jobs require cerebral skills and personality. This trend is continuing – one of many reasons why all young people should strive to get the best education they can.

Curiously, one profession that it is hard to automate to any great degree is shopkeeping / running a shop. I was a retailer before I became a management consultant, and I'm glad there are limits to how much the retail business can be automated. This places a responsibility on retailers to be sincere in their approach to customers. I return to the theme of sincerity, since the retail business has many insights to offer into the process of wooing and winning customers.

Increasing use of personal electronic tools tends to blur the differences between business time and personal time

More and more people use the same electronic communications tools both for personal and business purposes, whether for phone calls, text messages or emails. Similarly, they use the same electronic communications tools to surf the web both for personal and business purposes.

Naturally, this leads to a blurring of work and leisure time.

The increase in project-based jobs that make use of the skills you most enjoy deploying tends to blur the distinction between business and personal life.

With more and more jobs becoming project-based, your career success will tend to depend on how adept you become at putting your core professional skills to some practical purpose.

Other things being equal, you are unlikely to be good at some particular skill unless you really like exercising that skill, and if so, this raises the question of whether exercising it is work or pleasure. Especially if you like it so much that you are continually exercising it in the evenings or at weekends.

The best-known businesspeople exult in displaying the same creativity and dynamism whether at work or at play.

In a world where the cult of the business celebrity is more pronounced than ever it's significant that the business celebs we see on TV, hear on the radio, read about in the newspapers and on their blogs, positively revel in being the same business-minded, insightful, customer-sensitive individuals both at work and when they are exposed to the media.

I'm not suggesting that the personality they project to the media necessarily represents the sum total of what they're like as people. To take just one example, the world-famous businessman Richard Branson is known within the Virgin Group for his meticulous attention to the facts and figures of his various businesses. This seems to contradict his public image as a smiling, cheerfully competitive and customer-friendly chap.

Business celebrities clearly don't regard themselves as having a business persona separate from their personal persona. And if they don't, I can't see why anyone should.

No, you – and they – are just one person. If you are going to be customer-centric in your professional life, you will need to be customer-centric in the whole way you see the world and other people.

But that's fine, because being customer-centric in every area of your life is a great thing to be!

TIP 14

If you want to run a truly customer-centric organisation, make sure you recruit people who care about your customers!

No amount of commitment to customer-centricity is going to help your organisation maximise its customer-centric potential, unless you *like* your customers and *want* to give them great service.

People are at the heart of any organisation, and so an organisation that aims to be customer-centric needs customer-centric people staffing it.

Steve Lewis is chief executive of Majestic Wine. Majestic, which employs about 900 people, is today the UK's largest wine specialist selling by the mixed case.

Majestic Wine is a plc and listed on the AIM investment market. Benefiting since the early 1990s from the greatly increased interest in wine among British consumers, Majestic Wine currently has more than 160 stores in the

UK, three in northern France, and annual sales of about £250 million. From the outset, the business model for the company has been based around mixed-case selling: that is, the stores do not sell single bottles.

Originally the minimum purchase was twelve bottles, though the bottles could be any that Majestic Wine sell: the range includes wines, champagnes and spirits. In September 2009, the minimum number of bottles per purchase was reduced to six. Reducing the minimum to six has made Majestic more accessible to both existing and new customers and the company has seen a significant increase in the expansion of its customer base.

The mixed-case business model means that individual sales transactions tend to be relatively large: the current average is about £122.

At Majestic Wine, the nature of the business model puts a big premium on quality of customer experience. The stores tend to be spacious, utilitarian in appearance, and are staffed by people really interested in wine who come across as genuinely interested in helping customers and in discussing wines with them. The stores have wine-tasting areas, and the whole ambience and layout is arranged to enrich customer experience.

Meeting Steve Lewis is a pleasant surprise. One never quite knows what to expect when meeting a business leader, especially when the business leader is a retailer. After all, some retailers started out running market stalls and take a pride in their humble beginnings.

Steve didn't start his career running a market stall, but he did begin at Majestic Wine, his first job. After graduating with a degree in Modern History at University College London, he started as a trainee manager on the shop floor of Majestic Wine's Clapham store.

'When I started there back in 1985, it was the highest-turnover Majestic store,' he says, 'and it still is.'

Steve Lewis is understandably proud of a career that has seen him work his way up to running an enormously successful company. Yet he retains his sheer enjoyment of being a retailer, and still enjoys helping out when visiting stores – even loading up customers' cars! Steve aims to visit each branch at least once a year.

He says: 'At Majestic, we start with a huge advantage. We sell wine, and people who love wine love to shop for it. This means that when customers come to the shop, they're already in a good mood. Our job is to develop that good mood into a truly great customer experience. This requires sincerity, a real fondness for customers and, above all, staff who have the right kind of personality to do this job. That's why I attribute much of our success to our approach in recruiting the right people.'

And he goes on: 'My contribution to Majestic has been helping with the creation of a genuinely customer-focused culture. We really are a people business. Many businesses say this and don't really mean it, but we do. The problem with some people working in retail is that they don't actually *like* their customers. They see them as an interruption to their working day, and they don't get a buzz out of looking after them and giving them what they want. I can't see any point working in retail if you're not going to be charming with your customers and take a genuine pleasure in seeing them happy. Otherwise, yes, why be in this business at all? Especially, I might add, if you're selling wine, which is such a big, positive part of people's lives.'

'Over the past twenty years or so,' Steve adds, 'people

in Britain have become interested in food and wine in a way that was unimaginable in the past. The process has been spurred on by jet travel, foreign holidays, increasing affluence and a realisation of the sheer pleasure that food and wine bring to life. Nowadays, the restaurants of London are as good as any in Paris, and the British adaptability to the pleasures of food and drink has been part of a major cultural change in our lives. Look at all the TV programmes about food and drink. Look at how celebrated chefs have become. Look at the newspaper and magazine coverage of food and wine. We at Majestic love wine ourselves and we actively want to help our customers enjoy it.'

Steve also emphasises: 'We recruit people who love retail and who are really enthusiastic about taking part in it.'

Majestic have a policy of recruiting graduates. As Steve Lewis explains, 'When it comes to selecting our graduate recruits, we make decisions based on whether we think the potential recruit is a charming person who will get on with our customers and enjoy giving them great service. I don't think you can teach people to be charming. You can teach people to follow certain procedures, but charm is something they either have or they don't. You have to be many other things, too, in this business – driven, focused and intelligent, for example – but charm is absolutely essential and without it I don't think we can make someone into an employee we'd be happy to employ, or – and of course this is important too – who'd be happy to work for us.'

Steve Lewis even says he has a litmus test for Majestic staff. 'I don't want to recruit anyone I wouldn't want to spend an hour in a car with. That seems a pretty reliable and useful indicator for me. As for hiring directors, the test there would be if I'd be happy to have them in my own home.'

Steve explains that once he's recruited staff, he gives them the opportunity to enjoy their new career and to excel in it. 'Every new recruit immediately joins an induction course, and I'm the first person who addresses them. My aim is to encourage them to be all they can be when working for us. We don't incentivise staff on specific products, because we want to give them the opportunity to meet customers' needs from our entire range of products. And, from the very start, we build into our recruits our core philosophy – that we want our customers to walk out of the store having had a great experience.'

Retail can, of course, be an extremely stressful business, but Steve Lewis wants his colleagues on the shop-floor to avoid getting in a state that interferes with the quality of their performance. 'Our customers tend to be cash-rich and time-poor, and we have to be careful not to let any stress we may be feeling interfere with the pleasure of their shopping experience.'

He recalls: 'One of my formative memories working for Majestic was when I was keyed up one day and was helping a customer load a case of wine into her car. I thought my state of mind was something I was keeping private, but suddenly the customer asked me, "Are you always as angry as this?" It was a shock, and it forced me to realise that we can't hide our tensions from our customers. We need to be customer-focused without being worked up about it.'

Many people in business – especially chief executives – don't necessarily behave in a way that suggests they're putting their stated business philosophy into practice.

However, Majestic Wine's head office, located on an industrial estate near Watford, is an oasis of charm. Inside, its floor-to-ceiling glass walls, agreeable pastel-coloured carpets and general ambience are devoid of stress and full of calm, focused people – good-looking young men and women who like working together and who enjoy collaborating to give customers a great experience.

Steve Lewis readily acknowledges that his staff are mostly younger than he is. In a glass-walled meeting room, he casts a friendly eye at some of his colleagues down below in an open-plan office. He points them out, mentions what they do in the organisation, proudly emphasises that most of them began their careers in-store at Majestic Wine.

'Our staff turnover is low by the standards of the retail industry. We do our utmost to treat our staff well, and ultimately we believe that the way we treat them is reflected in how they treat their customers. Even when someone resigns, we treat them courteously and decently; we know that the way you treat staff who are leaving is taken note of by the staff who remain. Also, on a personal level, I can't stand rudeness.'

Steve warms to his theme. 'I want charm to be something that infuses everything we do at Majestic Wine, and I believe it does. We don't only want to sell to customers today; we want to keep on selling to them, and we want them to love shopping with us. And so we care profoundly about the customer experience, not because we feel we *have* to care about it, but because we *want* to care. I admire the John Lewis approach to customer service, and I'm saying this despite – or perhaps because of – Waitrose being one of our biggest competitors.'

Steve Lewis also emphasises the importance of teams in

Majestic's delivery of customer-centricity to its customers. 'At a practical level, when it comes to team-building, I'm a great believer in mixed teams – about forty per cent of our people are women. It's no coincidence that our leave of absence due to sickness is low; people come in to work if they possibly can because they don't want to let their fellow team members down.'

What about running Majestic Wine during recessionary conditions? 'The secret of running a business successfully during a recession is to run a great business *before* the recession. Great businesses do well even during recessions because their customers love buying from them.'

And what exactly does Steve Lewis, overall, see as his role at Majestic Wine? 'Undoubtedly this: *to set an example.* I want to inspire my colleagues to make Majestic Wine the absolutely customer-focused business I want it to be. The way we behave towards our colleagues, the way I think about our customers, the way I want the stores to be run, and the kind of experience I want our customers to have – these are all vital aspects of Majestic that I want to show by example. Selling wine is a wonderful business to be in. Every day I've worked at Majestic Wine, I've believed that this is the very best place where I could possibly work. I want everyone at Majestic to feel that, and I want our customers to know that's how we feel, and why.'

Steve Lewis's comment, *'I don't think you can teach people to be charming',* says a great deal – perhaps everything – about the approach you need towards recruitment if you want customer-centricity to shine out from every pore of your organisation .

I'm sure Steve is right. I'm sure it *isn't* possible to teach people to be charming to customers. People either are naturally charming to customers and willing to put effort into giving them great service, or they aren't. No amount of offering incentives or putting pressure on staff is going to yield the customer-centricity outputs you need from them, unless your staff are inherently disposed to be customer-centric *because that's the way they happen to be.*

So when you recruit, make sure your recruitment procedures identify recruits who are customer-centric and charming. Let your competitors recruit people who aren't!

TIP 15

Gather the kind of information you need about your customers and use it to their – and your – maximum advantage!

Start with the existing information you have about your customers. Many organisations have far more information about their customers than they realise. Getting new information is relatively straightforward, if you take the trouble. Examples of new information might be surveys, details of trading patterns, information you can get from social networks such as Twitter and Facebook, and, of course, specific comments made by customers.

Once you've got hold of your information, gather it together and make sense of it. Remember that information about customers is a gold mine. Don't look for confirmation of what you think about your customers and what you think they need from you and why they buy from you. Instead, be open-minded and receptive to new ideas. Understand your customers, and you will have a chance of being the best at what you do.

Remember what Proximo (played by the late Oliver Reed) says to Maximus (Russell Crowe) in the movie *Gladiator* (2000). Proximo, himself a former gladiator, is taking Maximus, his new prize gladiator, to Rome, hoping to restore both their fortunes. He promises Maximus the ultimate prize: freedom. As Proximo says: 'I was the best, not because I killed quickly, but because the crowd loved me. Win the crowd, and you'll win your freedom.'

TIP 16

Make sure you know why your customers buy from you!

Knowing why your customers buy from you is related to **Tip 10**: the need to know what your customers really want from you. But knowing why your customers buy from you is really knowing why they buy from you and not from your competitors. That question is of primary importance in your bid to deliver customer-centricity to your customers.

You've probably heard of John Galsworthy's series of novels that became known as *The Forsyte Saga*. Indeed, there is a customer-centricity point to make even in the title: Galsworthy himself did not call the novels *The Forsyte Saga*; this was a marketing ploy after his death, instigated to make the books more attractive to readers. As it happened, the ploy succeeded well; the books are still widely read, and two television series have been based on them, including the internationally popular 1967 series.

However, my main customer-centricity point here derives not so much from the name of the series, but from a particular paragraph in the first book, *The Man of Property* (1906). This book starts by describing an afternoon party at the Hyde Park house of one of the Forsytes. Galsworthy uses the party as an opportunity to introduce his characters, the roles they play in the world and their business successes.

In a rather fine paragraph about old Jolyon Forsyte, a senior member of the family, Galsworthy explains why Jolyon's mercantile tea business was especially successful:

> *Cigars! He had not even succeeded in outliving his palate – the famous palate that in the fifties men swore by, and speaking of him, said: 'Forsyte's the best palate in London!' The palate that in a sense had made his fortune – the fortune of the celebrated tea men, Forsyte and Treffry, whose tea like no other man's tea, had a romantic aroma, the charm of a quite singular genuineness. About the house of Forsyte and Treffry in the City had clung an air of enterprise and mystery, of special dealings and special ships, and special ports, with special orientals.*

This succinct description of what made Jolyon Forsyte's tea company remarkable is a useful example of how this sense of specialness came about. The tea became famous because of certain emotional and psychological associations attached to it.

This paragraph strikes me as being extremely relevant in the modern business age, when organisations succeed in developing products and services that are approximately of similar quality and technical excellence. All the same, some manufacturers or service providers manage to gain an edge in the marketplace by being seen as special and different, even though, seen objectively, their products and services are not any different from those of their rivals. How exactly does one achieve this specialness? If I knew the answer to that, I would probably be writing a book about it rather than about customer-centricity. It may be that being first in the market can give you a special edge.

Otherwise, it is really a question of how successfully an organisation presents its products and services to the public imagination. Sometimes a figurehead can help; who can doubt that Sir Richard Branson brings an extra special something to the many businesses under the Virgin umbrella? Sometimes the public's imagination is captured by a reputation based on some legend: in the past, the London retailer Harrods had a reputation for being able to sell absolutely anything, and while I doubt that this is still true, (go along and ask for a hippopotamus, and see where it gets you!) it contributes to Harrods' undoubted mystique – that of being the most famous department store in the world.

Some suppliers acquire a reputation for delivering quality and value, and build their business on it. For example, the travel and financial services group Saga has won enormous loyalty from its customer base for the quality of its products, and as a result has managed to create a sense of a community among its customers.

However you establish an edge in your marketplace, the sooner you can establish that edge and, more importantly, *understand* where the edge comes from, the sooner you can start enjoying the premium that customers will pay for what you are offering them compared with what is offered by your rivals. The precise value of this premium varies from one organisation to another, but there is anecdotal evidence that it can sometimes be as high as fifteen per cent.

TIP 17

Make sure you know how your customers buy from you!

This is a vital matter, because customers buy in different ways from different organisations: via different channels, sometimes via a middleman, sometimes on behalf of someone else, and at different levels of frequency. You need to understand the nature of the interface between your organisation and your customers, and you need to avoid being complacent about that interface, and also to be aware of ways of simplifying it.

Dell Computers, for example, is based around selling direct to customers. This can sometimes be a huge improvement on the traditional way of doing things. Saga's success is also based on selling direct, in its case to customers and financial brokers.

TIP 18

Remember what the most important sound is for anyone!

Dale Carnegie's book *How to Win Friends and Influence People* was one of the most successful self-help books of the twentieth century. The book was published in 1936, during the difficult years of economic depression and political instability that culminated in World War Two. It has never been out of print, though more recent editions have been.

In spare, direct, pithy language, usually prefacing each piece of advice with a telling illustrative anecdote, the book provides guidance on how to conduct relations with other people.

What it says is powerful, and was seen as revolutionary at the time, yet at heart Dale Carnegie's message is straightforward. He is saying: *modify your attitude to other people so that you can put yourself in their shoes and see things from their point of view.*

This advice is the essence of customer-centricity.

What great advice this is! If it were hard-wired into

human DNA the world would be a much, much better place and I dare say the history of human beings would have been radically different. Just how selfish human beings are by nature, and why, is a subject beyond the scope of this book, though I do address it in some detail in my book *People Centricity*.

Briefly, what I say there is that evolution appears to have made us unselfish in what I call a 'tribal' sense: we are not especially selfish in relation to members of our close family, and indeed, parents are notably unselfish in relation to their children. However, we are inclined to be selfish towards anyone outside our close family, unless the need to earn a living impels us to be unselfish towards our bosses and customers, or romantic involvement encourages us to be unselfish so that the relationship may prosper.

The trouble is that this kind of tribal unselfishness, which worked fine for our Neolithic forebears, does not suit the sophisticated societies of the modern world. These societies are linked together, in this era of the 'global village', by incredibly powerful mass communications and by our sheer physical proximity to one another on this small planet of ours.

I believe we need a more people-friendly creed to live by than the tribal unselfishness that has sustained us, often poorly, in the past. The Nazis, for example, deployed a kind of enhanced tribal unselfishness that extended only to Germans who fitted the definition of 'German–ness' according to Nazi racist ideology.

It's hardly necessary for me to remind you what the consequences of Nazi thinking were. But even tribal unselfishness devoted to one's family is inadequate in a world as socially complex as ours. As the newspaper columnist Christina Patterson pointed out in *The Independent*:

> *A society can't function, or at least it can't function very well, without the realisation that people outside your family are as real as the people in it. There has, in recent years, been a growing emphasis on the 'hard-working family' as the seat of all that's good: parents battling for their darlings' rights and now, God help us, even clubbing together to start schools. There's a name for a community that puts family first. It's called the Mafia.*

Realising that, as Christina Patterson puts it, *people outside your family are as real as the people in it*, seems to me the essence of what customer-centricity is. I use the term 'people-centricity' to describe bringing customer-centric thinking to everyone, not only your customers. For me, the Inspector's 'message' at the heart of J.B. Priestley's play *An Inspector Calls* (which was written in 1945 but set a couple of years before the start of the First World War), summarises the kind of thinking on which people-centricity, and its business world sub-set customer-centricity, is based:

> *But just remember this. One Eva Smith has gone – but there are millions and millions and millions of Eva Smiths and John Smiths still left with us, with their lives, their hopes and fears, their suffering and chance of happiness, all intertwined with our lives, and what we think and say and do. We don't live alone. We are members of one body. We are responsible for each other. And I tell you that the time will soon come when, if men will not learn that lesson, then they will be taught it in fire and blood and anguish.*

I wholeheartedly recommend *How to Win Friends and Influence People* as a highly accessible introduction to a way of thinking about other people in general – and customers in particular – that I call customer-centricity.

One of the most useful tips Dale Carnegie offers in *How to Win Friends and Influence People* is that for any person, the most important sound in the world is the sound of *their name*. I don't think anyone would dispute this point. It's a point that has enormous implications for any interaction with customers. I think some important points arise from this observation.

The more personal you can make your communications with customers, the better. Communications should not be inappropriate or intrusive, but they should be personal where the nature of the relationship between you and the customer supports this.

Over-familiarity at an early stage should be avoided. Just because someone's name is the most important sound in the world to someone doesn't mean you have the right to use it disrespectfully. I recommend that you observe the same formalities as people would expect to be observed in normal social situations, particularly when the customer service person is more than ten years younger than you. I don't understand why so many call centres allow their staff to address customers by their first name before the customer has given permission to do so. Many customers, like me, enjoy being asked if using my first name would be all right.

The next point is closely related to this one:

The use of the person's name should be sincere. Yes, by all means use the person's name, but do so sincerely. If you feel that the interaction has not yet reached a stage where you can comfortably call the person by their first name, don't do so.

One of many instructive anecdotes in *How to Win Friends and Influence People* concerns Dale Carnegie's namesake Andrew Carnegie, the great Scottish-born American industrialist. (In fact, when Dale Carnegie was born his surname was 'Carnegey'; he changed the spelling in 1922 so that the name would be the same as that of Andrew Carnegie, who happened to be one of Dale's personal heroes.)

In *How to Win Friends and Influence People*, Dale Carnegie explains that Andrew Carnegie (who was known as 'the Steel King') learned while still a boy that the most important sound in the world for anyone is hearing their own name.

Dale Carnegie describes how, later in Andrew Carnegie's enormously successful career, he and the railway magnate George Pullman were fighting an expensive war for supremacy in the railway sleeping-car manufacture business. Andrew Carnegie met with Pullman in a New York hotel and proposed that instead of slugging things out, they should merge their interests and create a new corporation together.

Pullman listened, but he was not convinced. He asked Andrew Carnegie what the new organisation would be called. Carnegie replied at once that it would be called the Pullman Palace Car Company.

That persuaded George Pullman. And from the second half of the nineteenth century through to the early decades of the twentieth century, the Pullman Palace Car Company became a major manufacturer of railway rolling-stock as well as streetcars and trolleybuses.

TIP 19

If you've made a mistake, admit it!

Few things annoy customers more than a supplier doing their best to defend some indefensible position after the supplier has made a mistake. It's much better to admit at once that you have made a mistake, and to hope that you can rescue the situation. Maybe it can't be, but you're far more likely to recover from the mistake by admitting it than if you pretend it didn't happen.

Everyone makes mistakes, whether it be errors of tact, protocol, or major business errors. Everyone experiences failure. There's plenty of evidence to suggest that even highly successful people fail more often than they succeed – it's just that their successes can be so dramatic, they tend to overshadow the failures. In the movie world, for example, many movie stars who are household names make movies which go straight on to DVD, or which aren't judged good enough for cinematic release in Europe.

Many writers enjoy initial success, then follow it up with a flop; this applies to musicians too. Andrew Lloyd-Webber (now Lord Lloyd-Webber) and Tim Rice (now Sir Tim Rice), spent some years unsuccessfully trying to progress *The Likes of Us*, a musical about Dr Barnardo, before Tim Rice had an idea for a musical about the Biblical character Joseph which in time became the global phenomenon *Joseph and the Amazing Technicolour Dreamcoat.*

When it comes to interacting with customers, we all have times when we're tired, stressed, demoralised and less customer-centric than we should like to be. Unfortunately, that is precisely when we are most likely to make a mistake in matters of tact or protocol, and there are no prizes in the world of customer-centricity for getting things wrong.

I think that pursuing a strategy of customer-centricity will help you get things right most of the time, but not always. After all, one can only be customer-centric if one knows for certain what one's customer's 'take' on things is: one can hardly be customer-centric if one doesn't know much about the customer. The early stages of interaction with a customer are likely to be difficult as far as getting the relationship right is concerned. Customers naturally tend to see themselves as deserving to be wooed rather than doing the wooing, so they are not necessarily motivated to reveal their agenda or what motivates them.

But even when you know a customer fairly well, it is still only too easy to be deficient in the tact and protocol you bring to the relationship. And just a single error in this respect can undo a long period of patient work to foster and nurture the relationship.

Being sensitive to someone's agenda is a human skill. In consulting, the profession in which I work, a customer wants three things: (1) the right service delivered at (2) the right price (3) by people whom the customer likes. The first two requirements should be relatively easy to deliver – if a consultant or consultancy firm can't get the price right and can't do the job, they shouldn't be in the business in the first place.

But getting the relationship right between consultant and customer, or between consultancy firm and customer, is always likely to be a big challenge, and the more money the customer is spending, the bigger the challenge.

Whatever business or profession you are in, you can never have a perfect knowledge of your customer, so you can never be sure of getting everything right. You may say something wrong, or do something wrong, without having the least intention of doing so.

My advice is, find out as soon as you possibly can what you did that has upset the client. If you truly believe you're wrong, admit it and sort things out.

TIP 20

Make sure you know who else serves your customers!

A crucial part of knowing your customers is knowing who else is offering them products or services that compare with yours. Until you know who your rivals are, you cannot possibly be customer-centric.

Many organisations spend more energy on belittling their rivals than doing what they should be doing – finding out what their rivals are offering and working out why it appeals to customers. You need objectivity to do this, especially if you suspect that a rival offering is better than your own, and most especially if you are right in suspecting this! In today's business world, where players operate under similar trading conditions, have access to similar technology and money lent at approximately the same rate, and must trade under roughly similar legal frameworks even if they are operating from different countries, there are fewer areas in which to make a competitive impact than might at first be imagined.

It's certainly true that in some countries – such as

India, China and Eastern Europe – average wage levels are lower than in developed countries, and this explains why some organisations prefer to site their call centres and manufacturing facilities there.

But apart from differing wage levels, the only significant differences between what you can offer your customers and what your rivals can, will consist of four major areas:

- the level of innovation of your product or service
- the extent to which your customer-facing staff are charming and friendly
- the design and presentation of your product or service
- the quality and the marketing of your product or service.

A good example of all these factors at work is the prodigious global success of Apple's iPad. Operating in a highly competitive marketplace, under the same constraints as its rivals and with the same opportunities, Apple – basing the concept to some extent on their highly successful iPhone – created the world's first truly successful personal computer 'pad'. The iPad was not the first computer of this kind, but it was unquestionably the first that captured the public imagination. The screen's ability to display any suitable visual, and the wide range of features that the iPad offers make us forget that in technological terms, the iPad is fairly straightforward.

The computer hardware inside the iPad is only a few inches long; most of its internal mass consists of the battery. Somehow, Apple not only sold the iPad to customers, but also the very concept of using a computer that was like a piece of paper. People have been thinking of designing computers that look like pieces of paper for at least twenty years but somehow Apple brought the ingredients together in a successful mix. They were unquestionably helped by the huge popularity of their iPhone, which won them a customer base amenable to being sold what is, in effect, a large iPhone with even more features.

What can we learn from this? Again, the more you know about your customers and what they want, the more customer-centric you are going to be. When a supplier is selling new technology, whether to consumers or to other businesses, there is a limit to what the supplier knows about the likely appeal of the new product. After all, customers don't know what new technology they want until they can see it and decide for themselves. Technology is perhaps a special case, and an exception to the rule that if you know enough about your customers, you can be reasonably certain that any new product you offer them will be moderately successful.

But all the same, a good technology supplier will develop an intuitive sense of what his or her customers want to buy, and will know what to offer them in order to maximise his or her chance of success.

Also, whatever you are selling – though this is especially true if you are selling technology – you can never rest on you laurels because the competition will always be trying to catch up with you and overtake you, and also what your customers want from you will itself always be changing.

In the case of the iPAD, for example, Apple now face the new challenge from the new generation of Android devices with five-inch screens.

TIP 21

Make sure that every three months you carry out a review of the reasons why your customers buy from you!

Change is at the heart of all life, including business.

Your customers change every day, in terms of everything they're doing with their lives, what they expect from their lives, and who they are. New customers come and old customers go. Your customers are continually being educated by other customers, and the effect of this education is that customers are ever more aware of their power, and expect to be looked after.

You can't just rely on how things were done in the past. For example, not long ago banks didn't open on Saturdays by tradition. But customers didn't see why banks shouldn't be open on Saturdays, and why during the week they shouldn't stay open until five o'clock in the afternoon instead of closing at three-thirty. Nowadays, the idea of a bank closing its doors in mid-afternoon seems preposterous.

You need to review your customers at least every three months; the review should include every aspect of what your customers are doing, wanting, how they are buying, what they are spending, and anything else that relates to their relationship with you.

TIP 22

Make sure you know, and keep on knowing, what five things are most important to your customers after they have bought from you!

This is precisely the kind of information you should be getting from investigating your customers.

I freely admit that the five is a somewhat arbitrary nimber. But I do think that if you can be clear which five things are most important to your customers after they have bought from you, you will then know how best to make sure they buy from you again.

TIP 23

Make sure you know, and keep on knowing, what five things are most likely to *stop* your customers buying from you!

This also requires you to have a deep understanding of your customers, possibly even deeper than in the previous tip, because, by definition, if you are investigating the five reasons that stop customers buying from you, you will probably need to investigate potential customers who are not yet buying from you.

In practice, if you know your organisation well enough and its interaction with your customers, it should be relatively easy to work out what factors are preventing potential customers from buying from you.

TIP 24

Decide whether you are trying to meet the needs of your customers, or their wants.

You can only put customer-centricity into practice if you can distinguish between what a customer *needs* and what a customer *wants*.

We need to be really clear about the difference between these.

'Needs' are the minimum requirements a product or service offers. A bottle of detergent for washing dishes is precisely that: a bottle containing detergent that has no perfume in it, no fancy branding – it is just a bottle of dish-washing detergent that meets a customer's needs for that. Similarly, an airline company offering a flight between New York and London would, if the airline company was only interested in meeting needs, simply offer the flight. Yes, the plane will need to be heated and have cabin pressurisation, but only because it's hard or impossible to survive a seven-hour flight from New York to London without cabin heating and cabin pressurisation; these are still part of the need. But there is no necessity for food or drink to be offered, or for the passenger's seat to be comfortable; these are not part of the need.

A 'want' is more about choice and aspirations. A want builds on the need to add something extra for customers: something that customers like to have but which is not part of the needs. A bottle of dish-washing detergent that contains a pleasant perfume and some additive that keeps the user's fingers soft, and which has a pleasant brand name that evokes the ideas of softness and freshness, and which is advertised on TV by a beautiful woman chatting to her pretty daughter, is offering to meet customers' wants as well as their needs. An airline that offers comfortable and spacious seats, good food and drink, and which emphasises in its advertising the quality of the service provided by its cabin crew, is focusing on meeting its passengers' wants as well as their needs.

Of course, in a sophisticated modern economy, an organisation that only offered to meet customer needs would be unlikely to achieve success when competing with an organisation that was willing to meet customer wants, too.

Wants are essentially an add-on to needs.

Wants are a customer-centric response on the part of the organisation to what customers really want.

To supply wants successfully you have to:

- know who your customers are and what they want from you and what they need
- where necessary, use marketing and advertising to

educate customers into appreciating having their wants met rather than only their needs.

A customer may say they want something, when in fact what they *need* is something different. The difference between a perceived need and a perceived want arises from:

- lack of information on the part of customers
- decisions made by customers based on emotions rather than logic.

As providers of customer-centricity, it is your job to know what the customer really needs. If you are selling luxury watches, you know that customers buy these because they want to feel they are high-status individuals. The same thinking applies to many luxury products.

What might be a want for one customer may well be a need for another.

What do you do if you are simply not sure whether what you are supplying is a want or a need? Usually the best solution is to aim to meet the want rather than the need. However, the answer could be as simple as asking if there is a direct payment for the product or service. If there is, it is much more likely you should be trying to meet their wants rather than their needs. Conversely, in providing a service that is indirectly paid for, for instance the provision of state funded social care, it is more likely you will be aiming to satisfy a need rather than a want.

TIP 25

Make sure you are using your own insight as a customer to help give your customers a great experience!

I always feel that one of the best touchstones of what customers want is our own experience as customers. This sounds obvious, but in the world of customer-centricity, just because things are obvious does not make them any less important – indeed, it may make them more so.

However busy we may be with our careers, we spend more time being customers than being suppliers; all the more so if we are busy with our careers, because for much of our working day we are likely to be customers as well as suppliers. All organisations have internal customers, and many of us at work are simultaneously suppliers and internal customers.

The heads of highly innovative technology companies could be described as customers during the course of their work, since they are being submitted new product designs, marketing plans, new recruits and other potential offerings.

Modern products and services can be highly complex; so complex, indeed, that an expert in the field from even fifty years ago would find it difficult to understand the product. Modern computer technology is often only really understood by the specialists who designed it; I doubt whether the heads of most large computer software and systems organisations fully understand their own products.

So yes, we are all customers as well as suppliers, and we should be able to bring to our work as suppliers our understanding of what we want as customers.

When we are customers, we all want the following:

- the sense that our supplier has taken the trouble to understand our needs
- simplicity and clarity from the supplier when presenting the concept to us
- courtesy and friendliness from the supplier in its customer service
- a willingness to listen to our comments about the product and service and, if necessary, to improve it in line with our comments.

We don't like our time wasted. We like things to be offered precisely and clearly and we don't want to have to queue. I mention, in **Tip 30**, the frustration involved when we are kept waiting by an organisation we are trying to contact via a call centre. Any manager operating a call centre who makes customers queue for more than a few minutes to get their call answered must be either a hypocrite or foolish.

After all, that manager, on occasion, will have to phone

a call centre himself or herself, and I don't believe they like being kept waiting any more than the rest of us do.

Too often, when we serve our customers, we overlook the annoyance we are causing them and don't consider how we would feel if we were experiencing the same annoyance ourselves.

This is, of course, a classic example of not putting customer-centricity into practice. We should be putting ourselves in our customers' shoes and imagining how we would feel if we were treated the same way we are treating them.

We should use every opportunity of drawing on our own experience as customers when we implement customer-centric strategies in our professional life.

TIP 26

Make sure you set a great example in how you treat YOUR customers and staff!

Most of us find it difficult to empathise with the agenda of others – and here I mean 'agenda' in a positive rather than the slightly negative sense that the word sometimes carries.

More to the point, on occasion most of us are hypocrites and content to remain so. Some of us go to places of worship and sing religious songs about living our lives in a way that we do not actually follow in real life. We are unpleasant, we don't care about the feelings of others – and yet we don't even bother to think about these negative aspects of ourselves.

This is a book about being customer-centric; it is not a book of moral improvement. But I feel strongly that you will never be customer-centric until you genuinely feel concern about the feelings of others and not just because they are your customers and you want to make money from them.

It is self-evident that no-one wishing to be customer-centric can hope to succeed unless he or she deals with their own personal customers. Indeed, the more senior a person is in an organisation, the truer this is, because the greater an example they will set.

One of the fundamental responsibilities that comes with seniority is inspiring others who are less senior, including young people on their way up the organisation who are learning how to behave. If you, as a senior person in your organisation, don't treat your own customers in a customer-centric way, you can hardly be surprised if your staff, taking a leaf from your book, don't treat their own customers in a customer-centric way themselves.

In many organisations, the way senior people treat their staff is a test of how genuinely customer-centric the organisation is.

When visiting customer-centric organisations, you quickly pick up from the atmosphere a sense of how the organisation is run and how customer-centric it is. You find a sensitivity to staff members, especially young ones who are still finding their feet, and you are often touched by this sensitivity, particularly because, strictly speaking, it isn't necessary.

Most of us have experienced working in unfriendly workplaces where, as well as coping with a difficult job, we also have to deal with working in an unpleasant atmosphere.

Any organisation where staff feel uncomfortable and unhappy does not deserve to stay in business and is unlikely to become known for its pursuit of customer-centricity. If staff feel belittled by senior people they are unlikely to give of their best at work and correspondingly are unlikely to be customer-centric in the way they treat their customers. They will see customers as merely additional stress and a nuisance.

I am not suggesting that because you run a successful organisation, you won't experience stress and, at times, snappiness. Sometimes the very excitement of being customer-centric and running an exciting business will make you thoughtless and perhaps more brusque to your subordinates than you might be in more relaxed circumstances. You can't be ultra-nice to everybody all the time, and there are going to be times when you feel, justifiably, that some of your subordinates are not pulling their weight and not making the effort you expect. In this case, you are justified in pointing out where you feel they have let you down.

But if you have been more brusque than you would have wished with staff during a time of stress and excitement, don't let the situation fester. Don't let your staff go home feeling that you are not as nice as they thought you were. You don't need to apologise for how you have behaved, but you can let them know, somehow, before they go home that you had to behave the way you did because your job is to make your organisation successful so that they, your staff, will have happy and lucrative careers. Tell them that sometimes, to do your job properly, you need to be more brusque with them than you would wish to be. Help them to see that your sharpness is, in a way, doing them a favour and helping them with their careers.

Similarly, if you have to reprimand someone, make it clear to them that you are trying to help them be more effective in their career, that you have a duty to maximise the success of your organisation, and that you need their support in order to do this. A member of staff who is the right kind of person to work at your organisation will understand and appreciate the time you have given to explain your behaviour.

Personally, I find that I need to temper my yearning to be customer-centric, and I need to treat staff well but with realism.

Sometimes, a member of staff is simply not right for your organisation, and after giving them several chances to prove that this is not the case, you are forced to admit they aren't right. Then it is kinder if you give that person the chance to work somewhere else where their particular personality and outlook will be more appreciated.

Be good to your staff. Be loyal to your staff. Remember that the way you treat them will in turn be reflected in how they treat their customers.

TIP 27

Make sure you understand how the supply chains in your organisation work, and explore how these chains can be modified to deliver a better experience to your customers!

You need to know about your supply chains in detail, and you should expect your suppliers to collaborate with you enthusiastically so that you can deliver good value and great service to your customers.

The American businessman Michael A. Folkes, president and CEO of M.A. Folkes Company Inc, a major supplier of logistic and contract management solutions in the US to Fortune 500 companies, believes passionately in the importance of suppliers helping their clients add value to the clients' customers. 'My organisation's primary mission is to save our clients money, thus enabling them to offer the very highest quality products and services to their own customers,' he emphasises.

The big secret of using your supply chains to deliver great service to your customers is this: *don't burden your customers with your supply chain issues.*

After all, those issues are not your customers' problem, any more than your customers' ability to pay you for your products or services is your problem!

I love John Lewis's 'Click and Collect' service that they run in the UK. It seems to me exactly how suppliers should collaborate to give customers a great experience. Basically the service means that if a customer of John Lewis orders anything from a John Lewis store in the UK or online, the customer can pick it up from their local branch of the quality food retailer Waitrose, which is part of the John Lewis Partnership.

The organisational infrastructure which makes this happen must be formidable and highly complex, but neither John Lewis or Waitrose bother their customers with that. The service is simply delivered to the customer with courtesy, efficiency and with the customer not needing to know anything of the process that enabled it. Which is the way it should be.

TIP 28

Make sure your marketing across all the key channels addresses the wants and needs of your customers!

Marketing and customer-centricity are so intimately linked that, if you are truly customer-centric in how you run your organisation or part of the organisation for which you are responsible, successful marketing will come naturally to you.

It could be said that, just as the basis of all life on our planet is photosynthesis, which marries carbon dioxide and sunlight to produce plant life, the basis for all great marketing activity is also a kind of photosynthesis – the marriage of customer-centricity with a desire to win more customers.

But this means *real* customers, customers who will stay with you and, in a real sense, *grow* with you as your products and services change to meet their changing needs. These are the kind of customers you want: customers whose lives you can enhance not only now but for as long as you are in business: customers who will be proud to recommend you *because they are happy about the impact you have made on their lives and happy to feel that their friends and relatives can also enjoy what you have brought to them.*

Pursuing a gospel of customer-centricity lets you market successfully because you are completely in tune with your customers' agenda and you care about meeting that agenda.

The reason why I have put so much emphasis, near the start of this book, on Professor David Thomson's ideas concerning the psychological factors behind consumer choice, ideas I explore in **Tip 3**, is that Professor Thomson's ideas get to the heart not only of why customers buy certain things, but *what significant difference the things they buy make to them.* In particular, Professor Thomson is, I think, absolutely right in believing that ultimately, the most significant difference one needs to think about is the emotional effect a purchase can have, especially when one is looking at the benefits conferred by different fast-moving consumer goods.

This, the benefit to customers, is what you need to think about if you want your marketing to have maximum impact.

But benefit is by no means an easy thing to analyse. I am not going to pretend that I have all the answers to the problem of understanding benefit: I don't. My only consolation here is that I don't think anyone else has the answers, either.

Let's try delving into the nature of benefit and see if we can break it up into its constituent parts. When we speak of benefit, what kind of improvements in the customer's life are we talking about?

Clearly, different products and services will address different aspects of the customer's life and so will cause different specific improvements. I do find it useful, however, to compile a list of those improvements.

So, I suggest that any of the following improvements in a person's life will be regarded by the person as a benefit. These are all *perceived improvements*: that is, perceived in the following areas of the person's life:

- health
- opportunities to rest and relax
- social confidence
- popularity within the family
- happiness and health of children, partner and other people who the person cares about
- popularity outside the family
- popularity at work
- professional status
- effectiveness at work
- financial position
- quality of holidays
- travel opportunities
- access to entertainment
- quality of car or other form or transport
- personal hygiene
- pleasantness of the person's home and garden
- sexual attractiveness
- overall quality of life
- quality of food and drink

I've set these down fairly haphazardly, and clearly some items will be more important to some people than to others. But it's a fairly comprehensive list.

Of course, your products and services are unlikely to touch all these areas of your customer's life, but they will need to touch at least one area of it if you are to confer a real benefit on the customer.

Remember that what I am talking about here is *perceived benefit*.

When it comes to benefit, perception is the operative word. After all, we rarely know for certain whether an improvement in our lives will truly benefit us. With hindsight we can look back and say, perhaps, that some thing or some change in our lifestyle or some new direction in life has had great significance for us, but it is almost impossible to know in advance. So all we can really do is rely on our perceptions. These are all we have to go on.

Living as we do in developed countries, most of us are lucky enough to lead relatively comfortable lives in which our basic needs are fairly well met, so when it comes to the benefits we derive from consumer goods, we tend to look for improvement on the margin – which is another way of saying that we know a particular group of consumer goods will meet our needs; types of orange juice, for example, will taste good and quench our thirst.

But we want more than that, and brand-owners of orange juice brands know this and seek to establish a competitive advantage by appealing to an emotional dimension in us. This emotional dimension, they hope, will tempt us to prefer their product over another one, not because it tastes of orange juice and quenches our thirst (all brands do that), but because *it also gives us some additional benefit or gratification which the others don't.*

For example, one particular brand of orange juice seeks to emphasise its freshness and association with the warm, sun-kissed lands where the oranges come from. This appeal to our emotions and imagination is a vital part of how brand-owners seek to emphasise the benefit their product – and sometimes service – offers us.

To take another example, for many years the vermouth Martini (whose advertisements have decreased in number recently) used to advertise using associations with young people having a wonderful time in a vaguely warm and Mediterranean part of the world. This association was very successful and unquestionably gave Martini a significant edge in the market. Objectively, of course, a bottle of vermouth is simply a bottle of wine flavoured with herbs that needs to be mixed with some other drink to make it enjoyable.

But this is the whole point. Promoting a benefit to a customer using marketing methods is not about promoting the *objective* nature of the product or service. The process of promotion is all about *promoting the brand as something that will enhance the customer's life, and the more you appeal to the customer's imagination, yearnings, dreams, fantasies and hopes, the better.*

Not surprisingly, this does not have much to do with promoting the objective nature of the product. And even if it did, who is to say that stating the objective nature of the product is particularly interesting or exciting, anyway? We humans are thoughtful and imaginative creatures, and meeting our needs – even for everyday products and services – involves appealing just as much to our thinking and imagination as to our basic animal requirements.

It follows that stating that Martini is simply a bottle of

herb-flavoured wine is no more interesting really, than stating that a Gillette razor is simply a well-engineered piece of metal and plastic. We human beings live our lives more imaginatively and thoughtfully than that, and the things that make us happy and which we perceive as enhancing our lives are the things that catch our imagination and which we enjoy thinking about.

J. B. Priestley's novel *The Good Companions*, first published in 1929, caught the public imagination and was an enormous popular success. It tells the story of a group of theatrical people enjoying life and travelling around Britain during the 1920s. It was a time when, to put it mildly, people needed cheering up, and while *The Good Companions* shows its age, in its day it was as popular as Harry Potter (given that *The Good Companions* is an adult book), and inspired numerous theatrical adaptations and movie versions as well.

Clearly, the fact that *The Good Companions* consists merely of two hundred and fifty sheets of paper covered in typescript bound together in a cover is not why the book appealed so enormously to the imagination and thinking of its readers.

Early on in the book, J.B. Priestley describes the working men's weekly treat of going to watch a football match in the fictional northern town of Bruddersford. In a powerful piece of writing, he explains why an objective description of something bears little relationship to its potential emotional and psychological appeal to human beings.

To say that these men paid their shillings to watch twenty-two hirelings kick a ball is merely to say that a violin is wood and catgut, that Hamlet is so much paper and ink.

For a shilling the Bruddersford United A.F.C. offered you Conflict and Art; it turned you into a critic, happy in your judgement of fine points, ready in a second to estimate the worth of a well-judged pass, a run down the touchline, a lightning shot, a clearance kick by back or goalkeeper; it turned you into a partisan, holding your breath when the ball came sailing into your own goalmouth, ecstatic when your forwards raced away towards the opposite goal, elated, downcast, bitter, triumphant by turns at the fortunes of your side, watching a ball shape Iliads and Odysseys for you; and what is more, it turned you into a member of a new community, all brothers together for an hour and a half, for not only had you escaped from the clanking machinery of this lesser life, from work, wages, rent, doles, sick pay, insurance cards, nagging wives, ailing children, bad bosses, idle workmen, but you had escaped with most of your mates and your neighbours, with half the town, and there you were, cheering together, thumping one another on the shoulders, swapping judgements like lords of the earth, having pushed your way through a turnstile into another and altogether more splendid kind of life, hurtling with Conflict and yet passionate and beautiful in its Art.

Today, when football is an enormous, financially important industry and when the 'hirelings' – who in Priestley's day were paid little more than a weekly workman's wage – are paid enormous weekly sums, these perceptive and poetically-expressed words about football are even truer than they were in Priestley's day.

The paragraph he pens about football has much to teach us about the *real* benefit of something: that an objective description of it has hardly anything to do with why people become so enthralled by the thing itself. Being a complex, mysterious and profoundly interesting species, the way we respond to the opportunities life offers us – which means the things we buy as well as the great primal experiences of love, Nature, and the begetting and bringing up of children, is tinged with a yearning to be the god-like beings we sometimes wildly imagine we are.

And that is the whole point. When we spend our hard-earned money on things, we want a gratification from them that takes us out of the ordinary everyday world – the world Priestley describes – and into a realm where everything is good, makes sense, and makes us feel a sense of oneness with the universe.

To come back down to earth, the more you can infuse your offerings to your customers with this sense of specialness, and can appeal to their imaginative yearnings *in addition* to the improvements in their life which the offerings can make, the more successful you will be in every sense.

If any of the above seems like wishy-washy or touchy-feely sentiment, I assure you it isn't. If you never lift your feet off the ground when promoting the benefits of your products and services to your customers, you will – literally – never turn in more than a pedestrian performance.

The type of imaginative association you are able to invest in your products and services when marketing them to your customers becomes, in effect, your unique selling proposition (USP).

As regards how you use USPs in your marketing activity – whether it embraces advertising (where you pay for exposure in chosen media), public relations (where you seek to influence the editorial content of media), or any other marketing activity that involves promoting your message to existing and potential customers – how you market your product will be up to you. But the main thing is to get the message right. If your message crystallises in the minds of your target audience the benefits your products and services offer to their imaginations as well as to their fundamental needs, you'll be on the right track.

TIP 29

Make sure you are effective in feeding back to your staff and outlets the insights you have gained about your customers!

Customer service is – at one level – all about feedback. When feedback from customers shows that they are experiencing complete satisfaction from what you are doing for them, you can be confident that you're running a customer-centric outfit. Of course, you can never rest on your laurels; customers will always want the service you offer to get better, but all the same, great feedback is deeply encouraging.

That said, most organisations don't manage the feedback process as well as they might. The following are common problems:

The process of giving feedback is often a nuisance to customers. Too many feedback surveys place unrealistic demands, time-wise. There is little benefit for customers in providing feedback other than feeling that they are helping to improve customer service. Many organisations compile feedback surveys (or have them compiled by outside organisations) that can take up to ten minutes to complete. However long the survey takes to complete, there must clearly be some perceived benefit to customers to completing the questionnaire. This benefit needs to be commensurate with the amount of time required to complete it.

*The questions asked are often off the point. Too many customer sa*tisfaction surveys ask questions that are ridiculous and/or off the point. The organisation ought to know enough about what kind of service it is providing to ask questions that matter and are pertinent to the service the customer is actually experiencing.

Even if the feedback process has been managed well, and the survey takes (except in the case of complex products and deliverables) no more than three minutes to complete, *there is not much point in conducting a survey at all unless the findings are going to be put into practice.* Haven't most of us had the experience of completing a customer satisfaction survey and mentioning certain faults, only to find that the faults are not corrected, and then, some time later, of being asked to complete yet another customer satisfaction survey, only to be faced with yet more questions about the same problem area?

TIP 30

Make the telephone a pivotal part of your successful quest for customer-centricity!

I've been involved professionally with customer service for about three decades, yet I never fail to be astonished at how bad most organisations are at dealing with incoming phone calls.

Mark McCormack, in his pithy and wise book *What They Don't Teach You at Harvard Business School*, declared that he would not tolerate mistakes being made in letters sent out by his organisation, because while there are many things in business that you cannot control, sending out letters (today we would say 'letters and emails') that are free from typos, spelling mistakes and grammatical errors is one thing you can control.

I agree with Mark McCormack. But why limit it to letters and emails? Why not extend it to all those other aspects of your organisation that you *can* control? Making your retail outlets more customer–friendly, for example? Transforming the way your staff behave towards their customers? (See **Tip 14.**)

And how about the way in which your organisation deals with incoming phone calls? Most organisations, even many otherwise customer-centric ones, are appalling at dealing with incoming phone calls. When it comes to making a phone call to almost any large organisation, or making a call to a small business I'm dealing with, give me the small business any day!

The small business is likely to answer the phone after only a few rings, and if there's no-one in the office right now (because the staff are all out, very likely being customer-centric with customers), then there'll be an answering-machine left on, and I can leave a message and someone will get back to me before too long.

Contrast this with making a phone call to most large organisations. I'm not suggesting that *every* large organisation provides an appalling telephone experience that ruins any chance of the organisation being customer-centric, but I'd say that many large organisations give customers a disappointing experience.

In particular, one of the main problems with call centres is the difficulty of accessing decision-makers such as supervisors. It's not impossible to access them but it's difficult.

All too often, call centre staff have little or no authority to deviate from a script they are given. This can make meaningful personal contact correspondingly difficult or impossible for a customer to obtain. This problem is compounded when call centre staff are in a different country. Large organisations often make strenuous efforts to improve the quality of interpersonal service their call centres provide, but as long as large organisations are focused primarily on *their* agenda rather than that of their customers, the chances of improvements here are slim.

When the telephone (or 'voice telegraph', as it was sometimes known in its early days) was first invented back in 1876, it captured the public imagination right away. The telegraph, which made use of newly-discovered current electricity to communicate information across greater distances than were possible before, had been around since about the 1850s, and the idea that it might be possible to create a telegraph system that communicated the human voice had teased the thinking of many inventors. It was a tricky invention to get right, and even though Alexander Graham Bell invented the telephone in 1876, the first such devices were not very effective, and it was not until the 1890s that technology had progressed to a point where a network serving a large number of telephone subscribers became feasible.

Since those days, the telephone has become what few can doubt – even in these days of emails, the worldwide web, and Skype – is the most important communication tool in the world.

That being so, why do so many large organisations fail to make the most of the opportunities the telephone offers for enabling them to pursue their goal of customer-centricity?

Large organisations in the United States can be worse than those in the United Kingdom at handling incoming calls. Many US organisations don't answer the phone properly at all. Instead, they use dreadful automated answering programs, which are all very well if you happen to know the extension of the person you wish to talk to, but make your life very difficult if you don't.

It's true that these programs usually offer automated access to a list of the names of people in the organisation, and if you know the name, then, in theory, you can use the system to dial the person's name. But in practice, these automated dialling programs don't always work well – added to which, it is likely that you're phoning the organisation in the first place to get hold of someone's name.

Many large organisations in the US make use of automated call-answering programs that don't even offer the caller the option to be connected to an operator. Basically, if none of the options offered by the system are relevant to your needs, you're stuffed. These operator-less automated answering programs give the impression to whoever is phoning that their call is not wanted. The thinking seems to be that if the organisation can make your calling experience sufficiently unpleasant, you'll give up and won't bother them again. Organisations that deploy such systems seem to have completely forgotten why the telephone was invented in the first place.

Scarcely less annoying is how so many organisations handle phone calls coming into their call centres.

In principle, the idea of a call centre is a good one. In the past, people went to physical, bricks-and-mortar buildings to interact with large organisations such as banks and utility providers.

Retail banks, partly for reasons of promotional visibility and partly because many of their most profitable services – such as selling loans, mortgages and insurance to customers

– need a face-to-face human interaction, have (mostly) tended to retain their bricks-and-mortar branches, though the numbers of these branches have been reduced.

Utility suppliers, however, are less dependent on promotional visibility and so they operate mainly from call centres that can be accessed by phone and on-line chat.

In theory, phoning a call centre should be a pleasant, easy, and customer-centric experience. If call centres answered the phone promptly, it very possibly would be!

I salute the efforts of call centres to train their often young staff in customer-friendliness. Generally, the quality of call centre staff is high, and while in the past call centres located in far-flung destinations (so chosen, because of the cheaper labour available there) were less good at handling calls in a customer-friendly way, this is nowadays rarely the case and many staff in remote locations offer excellent customer service.

My problem with the way telephone calls are handled is more to do with how long it can take before a call is actually *answered*. I don't know what your own experience of phoning call centres is, but it is a fair bet that you will know exactly what I am talking about.

For reasons I cannot understand, many organisations that invest millions of pounds or dollars in creating the call centre in the first place and staffing it with well-trained, charming and friendly young people, fail to grasp that expecting customers to wait for longer than a minute before their call is answered are effectively negating the entire purpose of the exercise.

It is frequently the case that call centres expect customers to wait for as long as 20 minutes. Why do they do this? Do they somehow think that a customer's time is of no importance – or, even worse, – that a customer's time is less important than theirs?

I often think that, at a more subtle level, call centreswhich take it for granted that customers will tolerate long waits, are actually exerting prejudice against people who don't have a hands-free facility on their phones. After all, if you're having to wait ten minutes to have your call answered, the wait could at least make reasonably tolerable if you could put the phone on hands-free and turn the volume down. But if you don't have a hands-free facility, and if you're on a mobile phone, you have no choice but to sit fuming for ten minutes listening to the same message over and over again.

And another point: if call centres *do* insist on keeping their customers waiting for several minutes or longer, couldn't they find some more ingenious way of keeping customers entertained than with a message that the customer may have to listen to a dozen times or more before their call is answered?

I don't think I'm just moaning here. I feel strongly that the following rules should apply when call centres take incoming phone calls:

Firstly, no-one should have to wait for more than one minute to have their call answered.

Secondly – something I mentioned in **Tip 18**, but is worth emphasising here again – when the call is answered, call centre staff should avoid inappropriate familiarity. They should only call the customer by his or her first name if they have asked permission to do so. This applies to all customers, but particularly to older ones.

Thirdly, while the customer is waiting in a queue, any automated message should be intelligent and avoid being repeated more than two or three times, even if it means switching to some pleasant music.

Fourthly, the call centre should work towards getting that one-minute wait down to fifteen seconds!

CASE STUDY

CUSTOMER-CENTRICITY IN ACTION: HARLEY DAVIDSON

Kick-starting a customer revolution: what Harley-Davidson's success in a tough marketplace can teach us about customer-centricity

Motorcycle manufacturer Harley-Davidson's passion for its customers, linked with the sheer quality of its engineering, has enabled it to do well within the motorcycle industry in tough times and maintain an enviable market share and profitability.

Overall, we can identify three guiding principles in Harley-Davidson's theory and practice of customer-centricity:

- Firstly, dedicate everything you do to meeting the customer's needs.
- Secondly, know and understand your market and love it.
- Thirdly, be agile in how you respond to changes in your marketplace.

The reason why most organisations don't win the love from their customers that Harley-Davidson do, is that they allow themselves to lose sight of who their customers really are and what customers really want.

Harley-Davidson knows its customers. As its website says, it's one thing for people to buy your products; it's another for them to tattoo your company's name on their arm! But that's exactly what Harley-Davidson's most devoted customers do. Harley-Davidson interacts with its customers at numerous touch-points: by phone, in the showroom, at biker conventions, in shops that sell biker clothes featuring the Harley-Davidson logo, and so on.

Yet the best and most comprehensive portal into the Harley-Davidson world is its website. The insights it offers into how Harley-Davidson sees its customers and strives to interact with them surely have implications for all vertical sectors – including business-to-business just as much as business-to-consumer – which are far removed from the world of motorbikes.

The Harley-Davidson website clearly seeks to be more than just a website that sells motorbikes. Instead, it's in many respects *a world of its own*. The website's design and content is all about enticing web-surfers – who of course include Harley-Davidson customers – into a motorcyclist-friendly world that, in its own way, is as comprehensive, coherent and comprehensive as *The Lord of the Rings* is to lovers of fantasy novels. The whole emphasis of the website is on paying homage to the culture and world of the biker, and is so sincere and imaginative that it's easy for the non-biker to feel it isn't a fantasy at all.

That's Harley-Davidson's US website. It's more expansive than the UK site, partly because the US is Harley-Davidson's major market, but also because the US and UK websites seem to be aimed at customers with somewhat different mindsets. The US website suggests that the dream of riding for hours along vast, straight, open roads doesn't have to remain a dream. It's the sort of dream that in many respects is hard-wired into the American psyche, just as we in Britain have the dream of chugging in a steam-train through a green rural scene. One of the many American spokesmen of that dream of hitting the road was the author Jack Kerouac, whose book *On the Road* (1957 – filmed in 2012) evoked an American yearning for the dream.

It is, perhaps, more an American dream than a British one. Certainly, it's difficult to imagine Kerouac writing anything poetic about being stuck in a traffic jam on London's orbital motorway the M25 in the pouring rain at seven o'clock on a Friday evening!

Yet, somehow, it's a testament to Harley-Davidson's skill in knowing what makes its customers tick – a skill that radiates from every pixel of the Harley-Davidson website – that any negative comment about the dangers of motorcycling would merely make the detractor seem a killjoy. The Harley-Davidson website is as resistant to bitchiness as American motor oil is to English rain. The danger factor may be different in America, too, where roads are long, well-maintained and often devoid of obstacles, and where a nationwide speed limit of 55 mph tends to make everyone drive in a sedate and calm fashion. Vehicles on a US freeway often look like a symphony of co-operation as everyone drives along at top speed but no faster.

Harley-Davidson's US website is entertaining even for people who are never likely to get on a motorcycle. The website also illustrates just how close Harley-Davidson's relationship is with its customers: one detects customer empathy and even a sense of collaboration with customers which implies that Harley-Davidson wants to nurture and cultivate their customers' passion for the road.

I also like the sincerity in the way the Harley-Davidson US website – perhaps to a lesser extent the UK website – relates to its customers. You feel that the people writing the website are as passionate about motorcycling as Harley-Davidson's customers are. This may well be the case: many Harley-Davidson sales and marketing people are themselves keen bikers, and Harley-Davidson tends to recruit people who have a personal love of its product.

And why not? Isn't that the way things should be? Customer-centricity is bound to be nurtured when as many people as feasible in an organisation share the passion and interests of their customers.

I think this genuine empathy with and real fondness for customers is, unfortunately, rather rare in business. It's most in evidence when an organisation manages to create a kind of 'club' element in the way it relates to its customers, so that they become less customers and more *members of the club*.

Another example comes to mind. This is the giant UK travel and financial services organisation Saga, which in its earlier days was known as 'The Old Persons' Travel Club'. Founder Sidney de Haan built up his organisation from a single hotel in Folkestone in the English southern county of Kent, by offering cheap winter holidays in Kent to elderly people from the north of England. Running his organisation as a travel club was one of many factors that won him the devoted loyalty of his customers. The eventual result was a travel and financial services empire which, when sold to a venture capital company, attracted a price tag of more than £1 billion.

Customer clubs can be highly successful, but like anything aspiring to customer-centricity, the clubs must be run with sincerity and passion. Loyalty cards and incentives such as frequent flyer clubs also aim do this, sometimes fairly successfully, although all too often you can spot the blatant marketing motive too close to the surface. Many organisations have specialised customer 'clubs': UK food retailer Tesco has its Healthy Living and Wine clubs, for example. Even children's books have got in on the act: many publishers have created clubs which children can join to get membership benefits, including special information about their literary heroes.

Harley-Davidson's passion for its customers, linked with top-quality engineering, has enabled it to succeed even in tough times within the motorcycle industry, and to maintain an enviable status and profitability as the last remaining mass-market manufacturer of motorcycles in the US against intense Japanese competition.

I think a substantial reason for Harley-Davidson's success – the intense loyalty it manages to win from so many of its customers and its operation to a high pinnacle of customer-centricity – derives from the brand values it shares with its customers. *It's not just the product that attracts customers to buy a Harley-Davidson motorcycle, it's also the fact that customers see the product as a reflection of themselves.*

The loyalty, even love, that Harley-Davidson customers have for the bikes and the world that the bikes evoke in their imagination, received a big jolt in the 1980s, when Harley-Davidson began to make subtle changes in the design of their motorcycles. These changes, they believed, would make the bikes appeal to a new generation of bikers.

For an organisation that has won success and renown

among consumers, changing the magic formula of its products does not seem promising. Very often, as the Coca-Cola organisation found to its cost, tinkering with products to which customers are intensely loyal is a dangerous strategy. But Harley-Davidson managed to retain its customers during and after the re-design process. The passion Harley-Davidson's customers have for its motorcycles is powerful and authentic. After all, what other organisation's founder's grandson – William G. Davidson – would spend time at Harley-Davidson conventions sporting a beard, black leathers and jeans in order to discuss the finer points of bike designs with customers? But if you think about it, isn't that exactly what a truly customer-centric senior executive of a motorbike manufacturing company *should* do?

It's the same thinking that has led to Maxine Clark, Chief Executive of the highly successful Build-a-Bear Workshop, the children's teddy bear retailer, having the job title 'Founder and Chief Executive Bear'. All the management staff in this company have the word 'Bear' in their job title!

William Davidson, known affectionately in Harley–Davidson as 'Willie G', was until his retirement Senior Vice President and Chief Styling Officer with responsibility for the styling and redesign of the bikes. He not only went into the marketplace and out on the road to meet his customers, but also to bikers' conventions where he met his customers face to face; not for him the artificial constructs of focus groups and marketing committees.

Remember the movie *Big* (1988)? Tom Hanks plays a little boy who is suddenly catapulted into adulthood. He finds a job at a toy manufacturer and becomes a star executive because, being just a boy inside, he has an instinctive grasp of whether a prototype for a toy is likely to prove a success with children. 'What's a marketing report?' he asks his boss, Robert Loggia, at one point. The Robert Loggia character replies, 'Exactly' – implying that he thinks his star recruit realises a marketing report means nothing when it comes down to what young customers really *want*. But we the audience realise that the star recruit does not, in fact, *know* what a marketing report is!

The most devoted Harley-Davidson customers know everything there is to know about the curve of handlebars, the look of engines, the design of an ignition system, and so on. They told Willie G how they wanted the bike – their bike – to look and feel. Davidson likened the process of communicating with his customers to being in the fashion industry.

The question arises: why doesn't every product or brand inspire the kind of loyalty Harley-Davidson wins from its customers? Doubtless there are many answers to this. It has to do with the very nature of what Harley-Davidson is selling. Bikers tend to be passionate about their bikes (some see biking life as almost a profession), and since bikes are the centrepiece of their passion, bikers are likely to be passionate about the manufacturer of their motorcycle. None of this means that Harley-Davidson has an easy ride responding to and capitalising on that passion. But it's hard to imagine anyone, still less a biker, as passionate about the utility company they use. Back in **Tip 3,** I suggest that it is easier to find a point of emotional contact between a product or service and a customer if the product or service is closely connected with the customer's leisure life. But even so, emotional connections between customers and products or services can be identified and made the most of, if one knows the customer well enough.

The real reason why most organisations don't manage to win the same level of customer love as Harley-Davidson is that they too readily allow themselves to lose sight of who their customers are and what their customers really want. As I suggested in **Tip 3**, you need to find out what really turns your customer on in terms of the products or services you are offering them!

The sad thing about organisations that have lost touch with their customers is that they probably were not aware of what turned their customers on when they first started up in business. Willie G often spent weekends with his customers, and I'm sure he still does, even after retirement. Do you ever spend weekends with yours?

This book is all about taking the trouble to see your organisation, products or services through the eyes of your customers. How can you hope to stay close to your customers unless you put them at the heart of everything you do?

WEBSITES CONNECTED TO THE AUTHOR

www.customersaretheagenda.com
www.stephenrhewett.com
www.c3-partners.com
www.customercentricity.org
www.vantage-partners.co.uk

Email:
info@customersaretheagenda.com
info@c3-partners.com

Twitter:
@srhewett